Living Life Fully: Knowing Your Purpose

Chris A. Legebow

Living Word

ISBN- 978-0-9952715-2-4

Forward

Often people think knowing God's will for your life is some mysterious quest. God has given you several things to prepare you for your life and placed within you natural talents and abilities. These are things you are good at and things you like to do.

Natural talents and abilities are indicators of God's special purposes for your life. As you pursue your interests and develop them, you will be making friends with people who have similar talents. As you discover what subjects you like best at school, you will be deciding what you would want to study further.

Knowing your motivational spiritual gifts will help you to understand yourself and others and help you to choose areas of service within the Church. The manifestational gifts of the Spirit are for you to use as you share Christ with people as well as build up the body of Christ.

This book is written to encourage you, strengthen you and equip you with information that can help you to make destiny decisions.

With Christian love and prayer,

Chris Legebow

DEDICATION

This book is for Christian teenagers, youth, twenty - somethings and thirty-somethings who are not quite sure what their life purpose is. If is for you if you want a career but are not sure what path to take. You may have tried school or work but did not find satisfaction in ether.   By learning about your aptitudes, your motivational and manifestational spiritual gifts , and developing them, your life path will be shaped so that God can use you to fulfill your destiny.

CONTENTS

	Acknowledgments	i
1	PART ONE: Living Life Fully Knowing Your Purpose:	1
2	PART TWO: Spiritual Gifts: Knowing Them and Using them	17
2.1	The Gift of Prophecy	26
2.2	The Gift of Teaching	28
2.3	The Gift of Exhortation	30
2.4	The Gift of Giving	32
2.5	The Gift of Leadership	30
2..6	The Gift of Mercy	36
2.7	Motivational Gifts Inventory	38

Chris A. Legebow

3.1   PART THREE: Manifestational Gifts   43

3.2   The New Song   44

3.3   The Gift of Tongues   45

3.4   The Interpretation of Tongues   47

3.5   The Gift of Faith   48

3.6   The Gifts of Healing   50

3.7   The Working of Miracles   51

3.8   The Word of Wisdom   52

3.9   The Word of Knowledge   53

3.10 The Discerning of spirits   54

3.11 How to Grow your gifts   55

3.12 Gifts Manifest in the Church   56

3.13 We Need the Gifts of the Spirit   58

      If you do not have a Christian Family 58

      CONCLUSION   61

      RESOURCES   63

Living Life Fully: Knowing Your Purpose

ACKNOWLEDGMENTS

All scriptures are taken from Bible gateway Modern English Version (MEV) https://www.biblegateway.com
.

1 PART ONE

Living Life Fully: Knowing Your Purpose

This teaching is about finding your purpose. It is meant for teens and youth (20's or 30's) who are uncertain about what career path they should take. It is meant to be a guide to help you in knowing why you are on earth. There is certainly a purpose for you to fulfill. Part of your purpose involves the natural talents and aptitudes that are in the core of who you are as an individual. Being a born again Christian you have strong motivational gifts that are within your spirit and the expression of them will help shape your destiny. Along with the motivational gifts, there are manifestational gifts given to every believer who is baptized in the Holy Spirit. These callings and giftings help you to live your life as an effective witness for Christ: God will fill you with His presence and as you use the gifts, people will be saved, healed and delivered. There are more in depth teachings on the topic of aptitudes, Spiritual gifts and manifestational gifts. This is meant as an introduction to help you discover the giftings so you can develop them and use them.

Knowing your place

There have been many young people in my life because I am a teacher and often a main concern is knowing what they may do with their lives. Although there are some who have a clear impression of a career path, many are uncertain and do not have the information they need to help them make wise decisions. This teaching is meant to equip those people with necessary information and knowledge as well as practical steps to take in knowing your purpose.

Ideally parents should know the giftings and talents of their children and encourage them to use them, develop them and make wise career choices. This is not always possible for many reasons. Sometimes parent don't quite know how to encourage their children in developing their talents. If you are finding yourself in a place where you are not sure about what you should be doing with your life, I pray this teaching will encourage you and help you by giving you information and inspiration to use your talents and gifts and make wise choices about your life. Knowing your purpose brings a tremendous sense of peace and fulfillment. You were created for a reason. That is the place I would like to start. I want to start with the origin of you on earth.

God created you and placed you in your mother's womb.

You were literally in the heart and mind of God before you were placed in your mother's womb. Your mum and dad certainly had a part to play in it, but ultimately, God chose to give you to your parents by choosing your mother. God placed you in your mother's womb. It was not happenstance; it was not a coincidence; it was on purpose; God placed you there. Those who have held a newborn baby most certainly know the miracle of birth. You are a new creation. You are a precious new gift to your family. There is a living dynamic that is present; there is something about you that no person could ever do – that is you are a living spirit, a precious soul living in a body on earth.

Psalm 139: 13 (MEV) You brought my inner parts into being;
    You wove me in my mother's womb.
14 I will praise you, for You made me with fear and wonder;
    marvelous are Your works,
    and You know me completely.
15 My frame was not hidden from You
    when I was made in secret,
and intricately put together in the lowest parts of the earth.
16 Your eyes saw me unformed,
yet in Your book
    all my days were written,
    before any of them came into being.

The word "wove" or the art of weaving hardly anyone does anymore, except for certain crafts' people. It is a special technique of taking lines of string or yarn and using a loom and placing on purpose each line of thread into the creation. It is an intricate and beautiful process that results in rugs, coverings etc. It is purposely pulling the rod across the threads so they are connected and interconnected.

Vs 14 I will praise you, for You made me with fear and wonder;
    marvelous are Your works,
    and You know me completely.
Vs 15 My frame was not hidden from You
    when I was made in secret,
and intricately put together in the lowest parts of the earth.
Vs 16 Your eyes saw me unformed,
yet in Your book
    all my days were written,
    before any of them came into being.

What the Psalmist is referring to here is the miracle of our existence in the heart and mind of God before we were placed in our physical body on earth. God knew you. You were created and God gave you the body that you are living in. God placed you in your family. It was a gift of God. Don't believe any lie that says that you were not planned; God planned you. Perhaps your parents didn't plan you, or your mother didn't expect you. Perhaps, there was some earthly aspect that was not expected but please don't believe the lie that your life isn't on purpose.

The scripture clearly explains in this passage that you were crafted; you were placed in your mother's womb by God Himself. That should give you a sense of worth. God chose you. He created the various aspects of your character. You must realize it was not happenstance. No. No. No. You don't just have to drift through life feeling unwanted or unimportant. The truth is you are so important, God chose you to be you.

Co-Labourer with Christ

The exciting part of being a Christian is that you become a co-labourer with Christ. Jesus lives in you and through you. The Spirit of the Holy God lives within you and helps you in all aspects of your life. If you are not yet Baptized in the Holy Spirit – start praying asking God for this gift. The empowering presence of God will lead you, guide you, teach you, bring things of God to your remembrance etc. The Holy Spirit prays in you and through you as you pray in tongues. It is an essential part of you fulfilling your destiny.

The most exciting thing about being a partner with God (Christians who have accepted Jesus Christ as Saviour and LORD) is God directs your steps and your paths. There are opportunities that God will give you because you are wholly committed to Him.

You are a gift to your family. You may not know it; Your family might not know it, but you are a gift to that family. God gave you as a gift to that family. The ideal is that you could build up, strengthen, teach help one another and enjoy your lives together as a Christian family. Family is God's idea.

God designed families on purpose. He commanded Adam and Eve to populate the earth with children. In the original plan, there would have been no sin, no sickness or disease, no death, no evil. It was God's plan.

God's plan was a Christian Family

I know that as I am writing this, there could be Christian young people in church that do not come from saved families. I know that because I was one of those people. There are special blessings on Christian families to help each other and to pray for each other and to use gifts and talents to help each other accomplish the best God has for you.

I was not born into a Christian family. I know what it is like to be the only Christian in your family. It is tough. They don't understand you. They don't agree with you. They believe you are wasting your life serving God etc. They don't understand us and cannot because we have been born again of Spirit and they cannot comprehend what they do not know. That is a good topic for a different series – how to be the only Christian in your family and live in victory for Christ.

The Miracle of the New Birth

If you have been saved, you know that it is a miracle that God saved you. I most certainly know it was a miracle for me to be saved. The mercy God has shown towards me gives me hope to believe that others will come to Christ. There was something – a gravitational force of love drawing me to God throughout my life. Never was it satisfied until I became a Christian. It was a magnetic pull of grace – I kept wanting to know more about God until I finally accepted Him as Saviour.

The Dynamic Pull

There was something about my life that I wanted God. I kept searching in different religions and philosophies but I was not fulfilled. I was searching. I knew there had to be more to life than what I knew. This could be a topic of study on its own as well. Some of you will relate to what I'm saying knowing that God drew you to Himself and revealed Himself to you so that you would be saved. Something in you wanted God. It doesn't go away as soon as your saved. It fulfills you to be saved but once you accept Jesus Christ, you desire to know Him more and more. You realize that only God can give you what you desire – more of Him. It's a part of the dynamic pull that will pull you towards God until you see Him face to face.

Let your own heart leap as Christ calls you, as He whispers your name, as He draws you to Himself: to prayer or to praise or to action. You've got to listen to the voice of the LORD. You've got to hearken to the voice of the LORD. There is some kind of magnificent grace that by a miracle, in spite of our own bumbling and fumbling, in spite of our sinful selves, God still reached out in love towards us drawing us to Himself.

God Places People in Your Life

God places people in your path. They may be your family members. That is God's ideal. It can be others. In my case, I can remember certain people who shared Christ with me, who told me about God, who showed Christian kindness towards me. He could send angels. Sometimes God does send angels to witness to people. Sometimes He Himself appears. It is rare but it does occur – He does share that He is Jesus. Usually though, God uses people like you and me – ordinary Christians who share Christ with others.

God uses people to help us find Christ, to help us find our career and to help us make decisions about our life choices. Usually, God chooses people. The person may come in your life at a point you needed to hear an answer from God. God can use strangers. God can make a path to you so that you undeniably know it is Him calling you At some point in your life, the miracle of the new birth occurred. You chose to live for Jesus Christ. Don't you know that all of hell shuttered at it. All the angels in heaven rejoiced as you made that decision. You made a decision that changed your destiny from darkness to light. You were born again. Any plan the enemy (Satan and his demons) had for your life cannot come to pass after you receive Jesus as your Saviour and LORD.

A New Creature in Christ Jesus

A whole new realm opened to you as you were born again. Now you have the presence of the most high God living within you. The Holy Spirit teaches you, speaks to you, leads you, protects you, warns you, comforts you. New possibilities come to you. You start to realize what you can do. If you come into agreement with what God's Word says about you, you will be joyful and rejoicing constantly because of the living hope of Christ in you.

Living in the kingdom of God, being a Christian, is living life on a higher plane. The focus of the earth is on what you feel with your physical body, what you want, what you think. There are limits to human life and the limits dictate what you cannot do. People view the earth as though all of life is their physical bodies. Living as a new creation in Christ, you focus on what God says about you in the Word of God; the highest standard becomes God's Word; Your priorities are connected to God and the things of God.

The focus of Heaven is what can you do and how can God empower you to do it for His glory and honour. God placed you in your mother's womb so your earthly heritage was established: hair colour, eye colour, DNA structure, body type, sex etc. God knew it all. The plan for your creation began the moment He created you. He thought of you with a good plan for your life. This is the special part. He gave us free will. We can make our own choices. God will lead us, direct us, guide us and provide us with choices. God will never force you.

God's Plan For Your Life

The plan that God has for you is an inter-active plan. That means you take a part. Your human soul (your mind, your will, your emotions) has an active role in what God is offering you. God wants us to rely on Him and to speak to Him, that He may lead you. He has the most awesome, most wonderful, most supreme plan for your life. Should you give yourself wholly to God you will most certainly know the mercy of His hand on your life knowing it is God who helped you, who comforted you, who promoted you, who financially blessed you etc. as you live a life of heaven on earth. What I mean by that is the blessing of Abraham, the blessing of the Mosaic covenant on you by faith in Christ Jesus.

Mature Christians may view their lives being able to convey the undeniable hand of mercy of God on their lives. You do not have to choose what God has for you. Jesus Christ comes to set you free from sin and addictions and hell and death. Jesus gives you freedom of choice. You can choose to serve the LORD or you can choose to go your own way, disobeying the Holy Spirit's promptings and offerings of God to live a life of heaven on earth. You don't have to choose God after He frees you – but what a fool you would be not to choose it.

God Celebrates your Birthday Every Day

I don't know if you ever had this experience or not. I am going to tell you that my mom always gave me the best birthdays any kid could ever want. She would ask me "What do you want for your birthday?" I can remember she always cared about what I wanted. Almost always I got all or part of what I wanted. Sometimes, I would want things that were too costly or not possible for a child, but normally, she would have a birthday party for me giving me a choice of anything I wanted to do. She would either cook my favourite food, or buy my favourite food. She would choose all my best friends to come. She would either buy me a cake or bake me one. She would buy and wrap presents of what I wanted. She celebrated my birthday as though it were the most important thing. She celebrated my life. I would have to be some sort of foolish person to let her plan and organize such festivities and then say – I decided no I don't want it.

That is the type of love I am explaining to you that God has for your life. You are God's favourite (each of us is). His plan is that awesome for you and your input is totally important. The very things within you that wants to do certain things, God gave to you. God believes you are special because He created you unlike any other person.

Some people believe the lie that God wants you to be bored, poor, religious etc. That is in no way true. Living with God is the most exciting, fulfilling rewarding life possible for you. He gives you choices; He gives you potential; He gives you talents and gifts; He gives you a desire to use your talents and gifts. As you do, you are rewarded with joy that cannot be described in mere words. You are living your life in the dynamic of the Holy Spirit and all things are made more beautiful to you because of it.

God wants to give you the very best; the excitements and passions of your heart God wants to fulfill. The desires of your heart to be given to you in Christ as you live with God's Word as your priority.

Ephesians 1: 4 just as He chose us in Him before the foundation of the world, to be holy and blameless before Him in love; 5 He predestined us to adoption as sons to Himself through Jesus Christ according to the good pleasure of His will, 6 to the praise of the glory of His grace which He graciously bestowed on us in the Beloved.

This scripture affirms that God has chosen us from the foundations of the world. You were in the heart and mind of God before the earth was ever formed. God knew you; He planned you; you were placed on earth for the period of your life for a reason. Some people believe the lie they should have been born at a different time. They believe they should have lived earlier or later. The truth is God planned your birth so that you could influence people on the earth during the life you are living right now. You were born in the right period. You were birthed at the exact moment you should have been birthed. You were brought into the earth by the right person. You were given as a gift to your family. You may say, my family doesn't think of me that way. Some parents do not know this truth. They may even say negative words to the child causing the child to feel unwanted or unloved. It doesn't change the truth that God chose you and your life has purpose.

Serving God is Living Above the Culture of our Society

Remember the truth that on earth we live in a sin stained society. If your family does not know God, they probably won't recolonize the gift you are to them. The culture of our world in North America is money and consumerism; the view of people is not always positive; your life may not be emphasized as important by others; sometimes people make judgements on others because of their profession or their financial status. You must know and believe that you are a gift God has given to the earth for the duration of your life.

Please remember God's emphasis is to celebrate you His creation. If your family are not Christians, you may be the only person that loves your family members and prays for them. You might be the only living witness of Christ's love towards them. There are eternal purposes for God choosing to place you with those people that are your family. If your parents are not saved, you might be the only person who prays for them.

I am saying God can use your situation, no matter what it is. God can make it the best possible as you give yourself to God. He can give you a divine perspective of your situation. There is a purpose for your life and God can make all things work together for your good (Romans 8: 28). Please know God will never force a person to love Him. He loves all people the same way He loves you. Even people living in sin, blaspheming His name, hard hearted and not given to anything to do with God; God loves those people the same way He loves you Christian. God always gives us free will. You may be someone special that God can use to show them Christ living on earth by your kind words and deeds etc.

Purpose

Purpose is not like a mystery box where you choose any slip of paper from other papers with careers written on them. Your purpose is connected to your gifts and talents and desires and likes etc. Serving God and living communing with Him is not like a mystery of what will happen next. The very qualities that make you – you – are what God uses to help you choose what you will do. This includes aptitudes, talents and gifts. You are Christ's beloved. He desires for you to know the desires, purposes and plans for your life. He wants to lead you in decision making. He wants your input. These things are manifest in certain ways. First , I will discuss the natural aptitudes that you have.

Aptitudes

I know someone that not only has the spiritual gift of leading worship but a natural aptitude for music. At the age of 3 and 4 she was playing piano and singing before crowds of people. She was singing, praising and worshipping God as a child. This is a natural aptitude as well as a spiritual gift that she uses for the glory of God. It has shaped the way she has lived her life and she developed it and uses it for God's glory today. It is also a spiritual gift and special anointing – but I am emphasizing that in children are aptitudes that parents should recognize and encourage in their children.

I also know a young child, this child at the age of 2 and 3 was showing athletic talents and skills that don't come usually until children are 7 or 8 years old. As a teacher, I was taught developmental changes in abilities of children. I tell you "that child" could throw a baseball with force and accuracy at a very early age. He showed athletic skill. He could throw a basketball. He had athletic skill beyond his age. His parents encouraged him and helped him to pursue his talents and abilities.

Perhaps you have aptitudes in sports, in music, in art. You like it; it comes easily to you. You use it; you enjoy it; it gets good results. Parents should notice these things with their children so that they may teach the children in the way they should go (Proverbs 22: 6). There are some kids mechanically inclined. They will take apart something and put it together again because they want to know how it worked and they could do it.

I was curious and wanted to know things and how they worked. I took apart certain things but could not put it back together. It was an unhappy tail of my learning but I learned about myself that I want to know things. I want to know how it works. I want to understand the reasons for something. That was in me as a 1 year old child who wanted to know how the game my mother and brother were playing worked. I wanted to participate. My hands were clumsy though and what I did is turn over the checker board. I wasn't trying to ruin their game. I was interested and wanted to take part in it. The desire to know things is part of how God created me.

Each child has specific qualities about him or her that makes that child want to participate in certain things, gives them a desire to try or to do something. Children express signs of their aptitudes as soon as they begin to use their arms and legs with coordination. I'm not saying it isn't there earlier but it becomes evident especially as 2-year-old children begin to explore their home environments. It is important for parents to notice what aptitudes their children express so that the parents can encourage them in those things.

Is it mechanics? Is it dance? Is it music? In a church, I once attended, the children from toddlers to teens and older would start dancing during the praise and worship. No one told them to do it. Yes, the parents would often dance at their seats. The children would go to the front of the altar and start dancing before God with all their might. The praise and worship was so strong in that church and the worship so free that the children would spontaneously start worshipping God with freedom. Those children had it within themselves to dance for the LORD. What is in you that you want to do in worship to God? Is it dancing or singing, or playing an instrument or playing sports?

Know your Gifts and Talents and Aptitudes

Write your natural gifts and talents on a piece of paper. What are your natural gifts and aptitudes? What excites you? What makes you want to do it because you enjoy it and because you can. It could be art. Some people are drawing and creating at an early age. My mother insisted that if we were to watch TV, we should be drawing or doing something else also. Sometimes she would sit and sketch with us; other occasions, we were given paper and pencil and instructed to create something.

Often, we drew every day. I can remember at about 1 year old, as soon as I learned to turn pages, I was examining my mother's magazines and picture books. Later, I would read and reread and memorize my favourite children's books. I started writing and putting words together in elementary school. I became a writer. I identified with writing words and love for reading. I enjoyed art so much because of my mother encouraging me in that area that it is part of my life all these years later.

Aptitudes that are identifiable can be developed. Children can get piano or dance lessons or be placed on sports teams that will help them to develop those skills and aptitudes. Students can be encouraged to play school sports or sign up for the concert band etc. I know that not all children have parents that make sacrifices to get their kids into developing their aptitudes and skills. Not all parents have the finances or the chance.

I have seen parents who sacrifice much of their lives to get their kids to music or sports events and training. These become core parts of the children's lives and help shape the people they become. It would be most awesome if each child had an opportunity to discover and use his or her own talents. There are parents who do not spot the gifts or aptitudes or their kids; there are parents who don't know how to parent or who don't know how to express themselves so they cannot invest in their children.

Even if you are a teen ager now and you love music or always wanted to play an instrument or do a certain thing, even if your parents didn't encourage you to develop these gifts and talents, you can start investing in your own self. You may like something and have an aptitude for it but it is like a baby gift that hasn't been developed. It is not too late to invest in yourself. God wants you to do the activities you enjoy because by your excellence in them, it gives Him glory. He delights in seeing you excelling.

Education

God uses our schooling to help us communicate with people and form relationships with different types of people and to learn things that will help us in our society. In Canada and the United States, we have free education in elementary and high school. People in other nations do not have this opportunity. We are given excellent education to help us learn our interests, and aptitudes and talents. School is a learning experience. Not just the learning of English and Math but also about how to work as a team or to show leadership, or develop musical talents. You learn how to be polite and respectful; you learn about others; the subjects themselves are a medium for the true essential learning of how to relate to the people in the society you live in. Sometimes, the only kind or caring words a child may receive come from his or her teachers or coaches. Sometimes the only role model for proper life is in the teachers of the school. It could be the only male parent figure the child ever has. God's ideal is that our family is nurturing and caring but it isn't always the case. Teachers matter to children. They make a difference.

The authority of teachers (and other adult authority figures) kind of scares me because we do have the potential to encourage and build up and cause children to explore and to pursue their dreams. But the opposite is also true. Unkind words can pierce the heart of a child and crush his or her self-esteem. As the scripture teaches life and death are in the power of the tongue (Proverbs 18: 21). Please, if your family or teachers or anyone in authority has said negative words to you, pray asking Jesus to heal you by His precious blood. Although words can be as weapons, Jesus blood can cleanse you, heal you and make it as if it never happened.

Some of these sports' gifts and musical gifts are developed in school. Often, they are. That's an awesome aspect of school as some of these aptitudes and skills are developed because the children are there. Sometimes, the parents make sacrifices to attend these events and even give further instruction to those children. Sometimes, the parents cannot attend these events but the child gets the encouragement from a teacher – parent figure who encourages him or her.

Developing Your Interests: It is up to you

If you know you are interested in sports but have never been taught at home – start signing up for sports in school. Explore your interests because God gave you those interests. It may be music. It may be helping younger children. It might be academic excellence plus any of the things I've mentioned. You have a choice. You can choose to use your gifts and talents by getting involved with clubs and intramural activities and teams at your school. Make the decision to invest in yourself. You don't have to accept that you never had the opportunity before. You have the opportunity now. You can choose to explore and discover and develop your interests. You can start participating. You might even become a coach for younger children or an assistant.

Knowing your natural talents and aptitudes is essential. As you develop these talents, your life is shaped by it. For example, if you were on a volley ball team from grade 4 or 5 to grade 12, you learned discipline, team work, essential physical skills, training, determination, sportsmanship etc. all of those things help to make you as a person. They form your character. Other qualities and characteristics are developed because of them. I am also talking about your intellect and the education you receive. You learn about important things in our society and discover interests in subjects and professions by studying them.

Education is The Way For a Profession

Don't believe the lie that going to school will get you in debt and it is not worth it. There are bursaries (grants) but there are also loans. I thank God for the bursaries and loans I got. Yes – there was a huge debt. It took me a long while to pay back my loans but I could not have the excellent job I have today if it were not for those loans. In an ideal world, parents have more than enough money to pay for their children's college or university education, but it isn't always the case. It may be costly, but invest some finances into your life. If you want a good paying job, a professional career, you are going to need college or university education. It is in always worth it to invest in yourself. It costs thousands of dollars, but every penny is worth it. If you can get enrolled in a university or college in something you are good at, something you are interested in, something that you excel at – you are in the right track going to college or university. If you are not sure what you want to do, please continue to read.

Not sure on a career path - Do an aptitude test

In high school, you have an opportunity to do an aptitude test through your guidance counsellor. It should be free. It will give you a list of multiple choice questions. As you answer, you will be making choices that show your preferences and that reflect what you are good at. Certain fields of employment that are appealing to you will be highlighted . The results of the test are an indication of your aptitudes and a list of possible matches for jobs you would enjoy doing will appear. If you did not do this in high school, go to the college or university career counselor and ask to complete it. It should be free.

All your interests are important such as if you enjoy working with people or like working alone, if you like working outside or if you prefer to be indoors. All aspects of the career are covered. If you are fluent in a different language – new opportunities are available to you. Your talents in sports or music will only add to your repertoire of things you can do.

Invest in yourself

If your parents cannot or did not support you concerning higher education – invest in yourself. God wants the best for you. The best for you is to be doing what you like to do being a productive effective light for Christ whether it is as a doctor or plumber or professor or truck driver. Please know that all professions require education and experience. The first thing required is the education. You must invest in yourself. Education is a way out of poverty or minimum wage living.

Paying your way through college or university means you must make sacrifices. Believe me I know what it is like to be a student with just enough money to get by. I used to live in a house that was so cold in the winter (no furnace) that I could literally see my own breath. Anyone who visited me wore a winter coat throughout the visit. As I sat on the couch, I would not only wear warm clothing but cover myself with wool blankets. My animals gravitated to me. We huddled together to keep warm. I am not exaggerating. This was not one year or two – this was for my 7 years of schooling and afterwards until I had the money to purchase a furnace. Even though there were sacrifices, it was worth it. Making sacrifices made it possible for me to become a teacher – something I always wanted to do. Education can open opportunities for you that will help to shape your future.

Start with a college or university program. To get higher degrees, things are built right into our educational system so that there are teaching assistant positions as well as grants and loans. You may not become wealthy as a student teaching assistant, but you will be able to make ends meet and have precious experience you can add to your resume, as well as the higher degree. Give it your best. Don't take second place. Aim for the best possible education you can obtain in the field you are interested in.

Aim High

Aim for the highest. Remember the high calling of God on your life. God has a purpose and plan for you; your clues to it are in you. They are the traits that make you unique unlike any other person. They will be reflected in the aptitude test you take. I'm not even talking about gifts yet, only natural traits that God has given you. If you are getting post-secondary education, you are going in a right direction. Please don't make the mistake many make. It is this – they are not sure what to take in school, so they choose what others are doing. They end up not liking it half way through the school year so they drop out and waste the 2nd semester. At least finish your first year. If you really hate it that much, find out what credits transfer to a different program and switch programs. Do not make these types of destiny decisions casually. Go speak to the school guidance or career counsellor. Learn about your aptitudes and talents. Choose your career path with determination and wisdom – prayerfully.

Standardized Test Results Don't Have to Stop you

Never believe you cannot pursue a career you desire because you scored low on your entrance exam or your Intelligence quotient test. I have met with teens who have been shattered by their test results and believe that obtaining a future in their desired field cannot be because their scores are not high enough. First, you could study and apply yourself and retake the test. Buy the study book from the Bookstore; apply yourself with determination and do it. IQ tests may give certain information, but don't let it limit you. For instance, I met a teenage girl who wanted to be a nurse. She was in grade 9. She was told her IQ test was too low to even try and to choose a difference career.

Determination

If you cannot get in one way, go a different way. Perhaps she could not start attending a university right after high school, but she could go to college and graduate with a diploma and transfer to university afterwards. Also, if you are studying and it is too hard for you, or you realize it isn't for you, choose a career that is connected to it; If you want to work in health care, research the possible health care jobs. Usually, what you love to do most is what you are good at. Usually, it leads to a career path that will be enjoyable for you and where you can use your talents to help others. Listen of you want to be a nurse and you don't have the grades for it, and are not willing to put an effort into your studies making them top priority, you most certainly will not achieve success. Effort on your part is required so that you may achieve your goal.

I have attached a resource for you from the Ontario Ministry of Advanced Training and Skills Employment pages.

Please go to the website -Advanced Ministry of Education and Skills Development (https://www.ontario.ca/page/ministry-advanced-education-and-skills-development) The website is rich with information about possible careers. Careers are organized into categories so you can see the requirements for assistants as well as professionals and managers in each field. Choose a career you could do. Plan for it and study.

If you are a post-secondary student, your main priority should be your schooling, not your social life, not even sports. You must make your studies the top priority. Should you earn an A average, you could win a scholarship and have your education paid. Make the decision to choose doing your homework and assignments before accepting social invitations. You make sacrifices but your future is worth it. Don't believe that the diploma or degree is the end of the path. It most certainly is an accomplishment and will open opportunities for you but you must be excellent in all areas of your life to not only get the job but keep it – doing your best as unto God. You will have spheres of influence that are unique to you.

Loren Cunningham and Bill Bright (1995) from Youth from a Mission and Campus Crusade identified 7 spheres of influence in our society. I won't talk about them in detail here but I will mention them so that you have some knowledge of them.

Family
Religion
Business/ economics
Education
Government
Entertainment, Art, Sports, Fashion
Media

I would want to add a category of Health care, technology and science because I believe it to be different that the others and it is a career that is in high demand. Each of these spheres of society have varying levels of involvement and number of people that are influenced by them. For instance, should you be a teacher, you have the potential to influence thousands of children or teens or adults in your career. Should you be an entertainer, you may have the chance to reach thousands or millions of people.

Spheres of Influence

Numbers of people you influence isn't more or less of your value to society. You could be a stay at home mom who invests her life in her children and grandchildren and neighbors and friends etc. She is not less worthy because she influences less people. The quality of your influence matters. What you do, how you do it and how you live before God each day matters. Consistent faithfulness, diligence, excellence, integrity etc. These character qualities and how you treat others with respect and Christ's love cause you to be a positive influence, a light of the gospel, in your spheres of influence.

Pray about the spheres of influence. Let God speak to you about what career you might choose and what would be the best for you. Upon graduation and entry into the sphere of influence or spheres of influence from your career, pray and expect God to use you supernaturally in your job. God can use you to shine as a light by your exceptional excellence. Most certainly you have overlapping spheres, your job, your family, your church etc. Pray over these spheres of influence. They are as portals to our social structure. They are places where Christ can be glorified because you are there living a godly life.

You are responsible for knowing and using your aptitudes and talents and natural gifts. Learn them; use them to follow an educational path that will lead you to a career where God can use you to effectively contribute to your society and enjoy your life while you are doing it.

2 PART TWO

Spiritual Giftings: Knowing them and using them – a Brief Overview

It is vitally important that you get your education and training in your areas of interest and aptitude. With the same importance, it is essential that you discover your spiritual giftings so that you can develop them and use them for God. If you do not know your spiritual gifts, you are missing a huge portion of your life on earth. You are a spirit; you have a soul and you live in your body. As there are natural aptitudes and gifts there are spiritual giftings that God has knit into your spiritual DNA. I am using the term DNA that is a physical reality but I really mean the essence of your spirit – the part of you that makes you unique that is in your spirit just as DNA determines your body. If do you don't know your gifts, you can't develop them.

I will briefly cover the different motivational gifts. For a more in depth teaching, please see other resources. My book on Discovering your Spiritual Gifts: Knowing them and Using them gives an in-depth coverage of the topic. This guide is only used to introduce you to the gifts and give you a chance to know yours.

Motivational gifts

Motivation is the thing that drives you. It's the thing you want to do because you can do it. It's the place you want to serve and connect with people. Sometimes, it relates to your career and sometimes it doesn't, but you may use those gifts in the work place and in the church. The gifts were given to us by God. God gives them to us to help us with our assignment on earth. I mean that your life has millions of possibilities. You will have millions of choices to make about your career, the people you are close to, the things you will do, places you will go etc. All of them are with significance. You are a light of Christ in the earth. You shine because you are Christ's: separate, set apart, Holy.

What matters most is that you live each day for Christ as though it is wholly unto Him. If you do that, live your life completely for God one day – do the next day and the next day for all your life. Your light (your words, actions, influence) will shine brightly in the spheres of influence including your family, your career, your church, your clubs, your leisure activities etc. Your part is live for Christ with each moment of each day. God gets all the glory.

Romans 12: 4 For just as we have many parts in one body, and not all parts have the same function, 5 so we, being many, are one body in Christ, and all are parts of one another. 6 We have diverse gifts according to the grace that is given to us: if prophecy, according to the proportion of faith; 7 if service, in serving; he who teaches, in teaching; 8 he who exhorts, in exhortation; he who gives, with generosity; he who rules, with diligence; he who shows mercy, with cheerfulness.

Develop yourself spiritually

If you were raised in the Church, the scriptures should be familiar to you and you should have some knowledge of serving and giving. Often, Christian parents help identify and nurture the gifts of their children. If you did not have a Christian family, you don't have to miss out on anything. You can invest in yourself. You must invest in yourself. You are only going to rise to the level that you let yourself rise. If you are the only Christian in your family, you most certainly must feed yourself spiritually and give yourself input that will help teach you God's Word and build your faith.

If you press towards Christ, there is no limit. You can run towards Him for all of your life long and never be at the end of pressing in. God is eternal; God is fascinating. His manifold beauty is such that as you begin to learn about Him, you always learn about yourself and His mercy towards you. There never is a point where you can say I know all there is to know about Christ. It is a relationship with God that started when you were born again and will continue throughout all of eternity. As I share these giftings with you, keep humble; be prayerful that God will reveal to you the areas of gifting and also how you should use them.

You are the Body of Christ

There is no Junior size Holy Spirit. There is no High school or College level Holy Spirit. When you received Jesus Christ as Saviour, the Holy Spirit came to live on the inside of you. You become a member of the Body of Christ. That means God can use you, whether you are a child, teen or adult. God wants to use you to show His glory in the earth. It isn't necessary done with bells and whistles. Let me explain. Some people believe the only way to give God glory is to do some heroic, epic type of deed or preach to stadiums of people or sacrifice their lives for the gospel. Although those things may happen to some of you, God cares about what you do in the moment by moment, day to day life.

As you keep in close relationship with God, God will speak to you, God will impress your spirit to give, to serve, to care etc. The spiritual gifts make it possible for you to effectively fulfill God's will for you on the earth. Communion with Christ should be continuous. The Apostle Paul encourages us to pray without ceasing. (I Thessalonians 5: 16-17) Some people believe it isn't literal. I believe it is. You can give yourself wholly (spirit, soul, and body) to Christ – not just once so you are saved - but you can give yourself to God day after day for the rest of your life. It means you want God more than anything. It means you may sacrifice things other people don't. It might mean that you won't go places other people go. It might mean you might not fit in with the current trends etc. It doesn't mean it is for all your life – God will always provide connections for you with people of like precious faith. But there may be seasons that you are alone or with a different group of people than your former self.

You must remember you are a member of the Body of Christ. Where you go, God goes with you. You carry Him on the inside of you. It's true the apostles, prophets, evangelists, teachers and pastors are the Church. The elders and the deacons are the church. But you are also part of the church. You represent Christ in the earth as an ambassador. You have a ministry: it is the ministry of reconciliation. We are all called to this ministry. It is a calling to share Christ with as many people as we can during our lives. Start believing what God says about you. You are the Church. How important is it that the Church knows how to function in the earth. You must realize God wants to use you not only in your future but now. Learn to listen to the voice of God prompting you. Learn to obey the promptings and you will begin to use your spiritual gifts. Developing your gifts comes from reflecting on what has spoken to you and how you have used your gifts and talking to God about it. Often, He will speak profound things to you as you serve Him by using your gifts.

Don't believe the lie that you are the next generation Church. You know Christ – you are the Church now. You have opportunities to reach people your age, professors, teachers, students, clerks, bus drivers etc. You have a chance to impact those in your life. If you work at a fast food restaurant, you can influence your coworkers and your customers. You can give the most excellent service possible at your place of employment. You can affect your teammates on sports teams; you can impact your friends.

You might be the only Christian any of those people will know. Your prayers for those people, might be the only prayers they receive. Please never believe your life isn't essential. God created you so that you could make a difference.

Sometimes, we are not aware of how important we are to someone's salvation or healing or deliverance etc. The reason is, God wants us to maintain meekness and humility. Remember it is Christ in you the hope of glory – not you on your own (Colossians 1: 27). Keep humble but keep listening to the promptings of the Holy Spirit that cause you to use your spiritual gifts.

The Baptism of the Holy Spirit

I believe you will not achieve your full purpose unless you are baptized in the Holy Spirit. The baptism of the Holy Spirit is not a one-time occurrence. Yes – there is a day you are baptized with the Holy Spirit – an occurrence but it is a gift from God for you to use every day. It is a prayer language that is the Holy Spirit on the inside of you praying in you and through you the perfect will of God. (Romans 8: 22-23) Don't believe the lie that is only for some people and not for all.

Jesus spoke to the disciples telling them to go wait in Jerusalem for the gift of the Holy Spirit. (Luke 24: 49). It was His last communication with them as He was ascending into heaven after the resurrection. It had to be important or Jesus wouldn't have insisted on it. As the disciples obeyed – over 500 hundred saw Him ascend into heaven but only 120 of them were obedient and went to Jerusalem to wait for the gift of the Holy Spirit.

Acts 1: 4 Being assembled with them, He commanded them, "Do not depart from Jerusalem, but wait for the promise of the Father, of which you have heard from Me.[a] 5 For John baptized with water, but you shall be baptized with the Holy Spirit not many days from now."

The disciples gathered in the Upper Room. They were praying and praising when suddenly God came in like a mighty rushing wind.

Acts 2: 2 Suddenly a sound like a mighty rushing wind came from heaven, and it filled the whole house where they were sitting. 3 There appeared to them tongues as of fire, being distributed and resting on each of them, 4 and they were all filled with the Holy Spirit and began to speak in other tongues, as the Spirit enabled them to speak.

They were overwhelmed by the experience and it has never been exactly the same. Over their heads appears tongues as if fire. That experience was unique but the Baptism of the Holy Spirit is for everybody.

The overwhelming presence of God was so strong on the disciples, they ran out into the street still praising God in languages they did not study. People noticed them and some thought they were just drunk even though it was early in the morning. Others who were pilgrims there in Jerusalem to worship at the feast of Pentecost, heard the disciples speaking praise and worship to God in their languages from foreign lands. They took special notice of the disciples.

Acts 2: 8 How is it that we hear, each in our own native language? 9 Parthians, Medes and Elamites, residents of Mesopotamia, Judea and Cappadocia, Pontus and Asia, 10 Phrygia and Pamphylia, Egypt and the regions of Libya near Cyrene, and visitors from Rome, both Jews and proselytes, 11 Cretans and Arabs—we hear them speaking in our own languages the mighty works of God."

Oh, please know, the same God that baptized them with the Holy Spirit, wants to baptize you in the Holy Spirit. The same God that compelled them to go into the streets is the same God that will compel you to minister to people caring for them. The anointing is for a purpose. The anointing is to equip us to be witnesses of God's glory. As we are baptized in the Holy Spirit, and as we yield to the Spirit, God will begin to use us in the gifts He has given us. You will be compelled to good works. You will be compelled to giving, serving, caring, obeying. That day the Baptism of the Holy Spirit, God's gift to us was released. It has never ceased.

Acts 2: 38 Peter said to them, "Repent and be baptized, every one of you, in the name of Jesus Christ for the forgiveness of sins, and you shall receive the gift of the Holy Spirit. 39 For the promise is to you, and to your children, and to all who are far away, as many as the Lord our God will call."

Yes, it is for you.

The promise is for all who believe. If you are a believer, it includes you. There is no magic formula or special ceremony. You pray asking God for the gift of the Baptism of the Holy Spirit. Quote the scripture to Him if you want. Praise Him and worship Him. Draw close to God. He will draw close to you. As you worship with all your being, you will begin to get words in your spirit that are not your natural language – begin to speak them out. God will not speak for you. You must speak. God will bring the words to you but obedience on your part is necessary. Use your faith; speak the words God brings to you. It may come as syllables. Like a baby speaking words, in syllables - usually most people baptized with the Holy

Spirit with the evidence of speaking in other tongues utter syllables and as they continue to do this a flow comes. I would compare it to drops of water, a trickle and a full flow of water.

The gift of tongues as you are baptized in the Holy Spirit, may come as syllables (like baby talk) but God expects you to use it and develop the gift. The more you use the gift of tongues, the more you will flow smoothly. Sometimes, God will give you the interpretation of what your spirit is praying. Sometimes, you will pray in tongues and pray in English back and forth. Sometimes, you may sing in tongues. Remember the Baptism of the Holy Spirit is a gift from God. God doesn't give gifts for no reason. The gifts have purpose and it is to pray, praise etc. in a realm beyond your human comprehension. Miracles, healings, deliverance, answers to prayer are the result of praying the prayers of the Holy Spirit in the language of the Holy Spirit.

As you are praying and praising in the Holy Spirit, spiritual gifts are released and activated. God might bring someone to your heart to pray for. God may impress on you to go serve someone or to give something to someone. God will fill you to overflowing but always for a purpose. The gifts are for a purpose not just a goose bump feeling. Yes, there will be a manifestation of His presence that will overwhelm you but it is so much more than just a feeling. God will impress to you how to use your gifts by impressing upon your spirit things to do, people to contact, finances to give etc. God communicates to you clearly and you receive it in your spirit – you know He has spoken to you. Should you obey these promptings, God will use you mightily.

Pray in Tongues and the Gift of Tongues

God gave you the gift to use. Start praying in tongues each day. Make it part of your prayer because it is the prayer language God gave us. Pray in tongues in church. Praise in tongues. Praying in tongues builds up and strengthens your inner man.

If you speak out loud in tongues in Church – it is a special gifting of the gift of tongues (discussed more in the next section) given to the congregation. If you are not sure you should – don't. Become familiar with the voice of God before you speak it out. The gift of tongues for the church is always followed by an interpretation of tongues. It might be you yourself or it might be someone else.

The Gift of Prophecy

Usually with this gift it comes during the praise and worship or after the service or at the altar. It usually is connected to praise and worship and waiting on the LORD to speak. It is a prompting that God wants you to speak these words. It could be a scripture. It could be a song. It is always given for the building up of the church. It is also a sign to visitors that God is living in us.

The main function of prophecy in church is as follows:

I Corinthians 14: 3 But he who prophesies speaks to men for their edification and exhortation and comfort.

Edification – building up, teaching, strengthening
Exhortation – encouragement
Comfort – special words from God for that congregation that cause the local body of Christ to be comforted.

Acts 2: 24 But if all prophesy and there comes in one who does not believe or one unlearned, he is convinced by all and judged by all. 25 Thus the secrets of his heart are revealed. And so falling down on his face, he will worship God and report that God is truly among you.

A former Pastor of mine was also a mighty Prophet of God. He would be preaching and speak a word of prophecy and people would go kneel at the altar weeping. Sometimes, he called them out and prophesied over them; other times, it was a word for the church and people would respond usually overwhelmed at knowing that God was directly speaking to them through the Pastor. He was not only using the gift of prophesy but has the ministry gift of Prophet and speaks words that warn, release gifting and callings, correction as well as words of wisdom and words of knowledge very strong.

Using your gifts faithfully will always connect you to others who are like minded - people of like precious faith – people who believe the same as you. Some will become your teachers and mentors. Some will become your friends. Some you will teach and mentor. God uses members of the Body of Christ to disciple other members of the Body of Christ.

The Presence of God is for the Whole Family

Sometimes, in church service the Spirit of God would move so mightily through the praise and worship, people were praising God in tongues and the gifts of the Spirit would be manifest mightily. People would go forward into the altar area. Sometimes dancing, sometimes weeping, sometimes falling prostrate on the ground to worship not even lifting their eyes. No one had to explain to the children what was going on. The children would often go dance before God. Children would know God was speaking to their mother or their dad because of the parent was lying on the carpet worshipping God; the children knew the presence of God. They were not strangers to it. They could sense the beautiful presence of Jesus. I've seen families with children come and the parents would place the kids on a blanket and give them books and toys as they went to the front to worship God.

Children raised in such a presence of God, will seek the LORD as their priority. They will know God at an early age. They will give themselves as they see their parents and the other adults worshipping, praising and using the gifts of the Spirit.

Testimony of Receiving Prophetic Word

Once, it was many years ago, I was trying to get a job as a teacher and there were no jobs. I was making minimum wage with student loan debt and feeling overwhelmed that there wasn't an opportunity for me. I remember praying on the way to church, asking God to answer my prayer about a job. I knew God heard me. I knew that I knew His presence was so on me in that car. As I got to church I sat in the front row (as usual) and a child – a boy, the son of a woman I knew came to me and sat next to me. This is unusual. Children usually sit with their parents. He and his sister were talking to me about the panda bears at the Toledo zoo. I had wanted to go, but money was an obstacle. I made some kind conversation with them.

Suddenly the boy spoke to me and said I want to give you this sticker (from the Toledo Zoo – a panda bear). I hesitated. He spoke and said God cares about you and you will get your job. There was that miracle child of about 9 years old who obeyed God's prompting and comforted me. As he spoke those words to me, I knew that I knew only God could be speaking to me. My heart rejoiced. The children went to sit with their parents. Within 2 weeks I had a job. I fully believe that boy's obedience to God made a tremendous difference in my life. God can use you, but you must obey.

If these things I am speaking to you seem strange and you have never known about them but you are going to a full gospel Church (believing in the gifts of the Spirit) it is not a good sign. It means the gifts are not flowing in your church. You need to pray for revival. In some instances, you need to get out of that church and go where you know God's Spirit is evident. How will you know? The gifts of the Spirit and the fruit of the Spirit will be manifest. People will be getting saved, healed, delivered. People's lives will be transformed. There will be testimonies of people who God has healed and done miracles for. Usually the place is thriving with people sitting in overflow rooms because the sanctuary is full.

If you do not know the atmosphere for the Holy Spirit as I've described, decide yourself to go to meetings and Crusades and events where people worship and praise Christ in abandonment. There is Christian media that can make a big impact on your life. There are preachers and teachers of faith and Spirit who you can listen to or watch. There are conferences where the presence of God is so strong you will be released into the glory realms of God. Media is not as good as in person but would still be worth it. Never settle than less of what God has for you. God wants you to live in the Spirit. You must be with people who believe the same as you to get the benefits of the gifts of the Spirit. Your using your gifts is important but so is others using their gifts. You receive. You give. You are a part of the Body of Christ – a living member . The technology of the Internet, Satellite and TV make it possible for us to get excellence from throughout the world.

Gifts of the Spirit are Evidence of a Living Church

The local church should be a place where the spiritual gifts flow freely. The gift of tongues and interpretation and prophecy should regularly be in our meetings. The gifts of the Spirit manifest are a sign of life. The gift of faith can be so strong in a congregation that you all agree in prayer together, I mean in the sanctuary, you all agree in faith and miracles are manifest. The gift of miracles and gifts of healing should be evident in the Church. The word of God will be preached about healing and healings will occur. People will want to come to your church because they know there is something supernatural going on there. Churches that manifest the presence of God with healings and miracles and the other gifts of the Spirit, are crowded. People want to go to these services. There is no problem with church attendance.

Church is not a building or a service that we go to. It is the dynamic that we live in. There is healing. There is salvation. There is deliverance. If you don't know that church can be exciting, please know – it can be. God's presence is the reason we gather together. We are the Body of Christ on the earth. As we gather together, God's Holy presence comes in the midst of us and should we let the Holy Spirit move through us, the miraculous will be manifest.

Matthew 18: 19 "Again I say to you, that if two of you agree on earth about anything they ask, it will be done for them by My Father who is in heaven. 20 For where two or three are assembled in My name, there I am in their midst."

I've got some places I could recommend to you. I've got some ministries I could invite you to listen to or watch. There is a living, dynamic charismatic church on the earth that is flourishing. The glory of God in The Church is not a thing of the past. You can be a vessel God uses to bring salvation or healing or deliverance to someone. It is your willingness and obedience to the Holy Spirit that makes it possible for God to use you. God using you can transform someone's life.

The Gift of Prophecy

The gift of prophesy is someone who gets a prompting in his or her spirit to speak a word from God. It should occur regularly in our Church services but is not confined to our church services. It can occur in small group meetings or at school or at work etc. Prophesy for the church will occur in church meetings. It is to build up, encourage and strengthen the local church. God can give you specific prophetic words to speak to people outside of the church also. The purpose is the same: to build up encourage and strengthen the person.

God literally impresses on your spirit to say words that encourage, exhort, comfort or build up someone else. You will feel an inner prompting to share the word. Often the gift of words of wisdom and word of knowledge are evident also and they together make an effective word of encouragement. If you feel a prompting to speak, obey and speak it out. If you are not sure you should say it – don't. Rather, after the service go to the Pastor and share it with him or her. That pastor should give you direction in using your gifts. Often God will quicken a scripture to you and you should speak it. There could be someone who needed to hear that exact word. If you have not taken a Spiritual Gifts Inventory I want to highly recommend that you use mine. Your church mostly likely has its own. If possible, attend the class on Spiritual gifts so that you get more in depth teaching. It will help you to understand yourself and others.

Romans 12: 6 We have diverse gifts according to the grace that is given to us: if prophecy, according to the proportion of faith;

Prophesy with faith believing the words you are saying will encourage, build up, strengthen and release faith in the people you are speaking to. You can be praying and prophesying as you pray in your private life. The gift of prophesy is for you to use at home, at church, in all places of your life. Pray for wisdom to use the gift as you should. If you know of a prophet in your church, someone who regularly prophesies, try to learn from him or her. Also, if you are at all uncertain, speak with your pastor about it. There are places in the service that are natural pauses and chances for prophesy to be released. It usually is during or right after the praise in worship or at the end of the service or in the altar call. It is not disruptive. Never do you interrupt someone who is already speaking.

1 Corinthians 14: 40 Let all things be done decently and in order.

Serving

Serving people in practical ways is using this gift. This would include child care, serving food or washing dishes or mowing someone's lawn. It includes all these things that don't seem spiritual. God uses servants to be the hands of Christ on the earth, your giving of your time, your talents and your efforts are all parts of this gift. You could be serving in the church building such as deacons or chefs or ushers etc. You might also feel a strong prompting in your spirit (it is a spiritual gift) to help a neighbour or a total stronger. You may help someone carry groceries or lift an object, or move furniture. It may not seem spiritual to you but it is spiritual. Your obedience could mean a true blessing to someone's life. It releases thanksgiving and often frees someone who could not do that thing. It can include things such as baking or cooking for people. Because there is such a strong need for this gift in the church, there are often many people with the gift of serving.

In one of my former churches, there is a club of youth and teens and mostly men who volunteered to go help widows and single parents by shoveling snow, mowing the lawn, doing repairs around the home etc. They were true deacons – or servants even though not all of them had the title of deacon. You will know if you are a servant because you will enjoy doing things for people.

The gift of serving is often used as a method for evangelism. Churches host events and dinners for people to share Christ with them. There are churches who offer free car washes. Some churches and para church organizations (Christian Ministries) help clean, rebuild and care for their homes and property after a natural disaster.

Children can start serving by helping their parents not only in the home but in their ministry in church. New believers are usually very enthusiastic and full of passion for God. They would make excellent greeters or ushers because they would do it with enthusiasm. They could help in the kitchen or serving tables or cleaning. There is a place for new believers; it's not teaching in the pulpit but could be serving.

Teenagers and those in their 20's and 30's should be able to be ushers or greeters. It should be possible for the youth to run the service with somebody leading worship, somebody praying, ushers, someone sharing the word. By giving teens experience doing these things, they will begin to know their gifts and callings. You may start donating to usher and find you like it so much you do it for many years.

Be pure in heart as you serve. Do it as unto the LORD. Give your best possible. Be faithful in what you do. Do it for Christ.

Teaching

The teacher is somebody who takes notes in church. You will see people with pads of paper or writing tablets, carefully copying the main points of the Pastor's sermon. Sometimes, these people go home and reread the notes or lookup the scriptures. The Pastor almost always highlight key points in his or her sermon. The teacher will try to absorb these truths not only by listening but by writing them. Sometimes, they will study in depth all aspects of one scripture mentioned. The teacher is someone who wants to learn all he or she can during his or her life.

Teachers love to learn

The teacher will often own a study Bible or several different translations including a Greek/Hebrew concordance. I remember I was so excited to get a New Testament that had 7 different translations of the scripture side by side. It was a multi translation line by line Bible. On the Internet now, there are so many excellent resources. There are different commentaries, translations of more than 20 versions and in different languages, concordances etc. available for free. I thank God for the different study helps and translations available at the click of a mouse. We can use these things for the glory of God.

Commentaries are books by people writing their options and interpretations of the Scripture. They can be an excellent study help. Always remember it is not the Bible itself but a person's interpretation. Some of them are anointed and some of them aren't. Take the good and disregard that which is not helpful. The highest authority is not the commentary writer or even a pastor. The Highest authority is God's Word.

Pray as you read and study the Bible and God will show you gems or precious aspects of His Word through the Holy Spirit. The Holy Spirit is our Teacher. The Holy Spirit inspired godly men to record the Word of God. It is the same Holy Spirit that can quicken these truths to you.

The teacher likes to dig in the Word of God. This may include reading commentaries and historical documents that explain and add understanding to the Bible. The teacher will always compare scriptures with scriptures. The teacher likes to know the original Hebrew and Greek meanings of key words. The teacher loves to study and loves to discuss scripture. They love to share what they have learned and learn from others. The teacher enjoys teaching the Word of God. It may be to one person or to a small group, or to large groups or even congregations. There are teenagers at my church who love to use their teaching gift by helping to teach the children. As the teacher uses the teaching gift, it releases joy as it is his or her passion to do.

As the teacher uses his or her teaching gift, he or she is learning. God always gives more revelation and insight to the teacher than he or she can possibly express. As you pour out, God gives you more. Revelation, insight, knowledge come to the teacher studying the Word as the Holy Spirit quickens the Word of God and helps the person to organize information into chunks or lessons or teaching units.

Most Teachers are Shy

Sometimes the teachers are very shy and they hesitate to speak in public. They do the studying and preparation for sermons at home, but don't want to stand up in front of people. Oral presentation and teaching is learned. Should an older teacher mentor a younger one, things such as voice tone, explanation and projection and body posture – all these aspects of presenting can be learned. Hopefully, God will place teachers in your life so that you can learn from them in your local church. It is not true that you are not meant to share your gift because of fear of people. You may teach to one person, or a small group or a large group. God gave you the gift of teaching because He wants you to use it. It is good that you are digging nuggets from God's Word but it isn't so that you keep it to yourself.

The teacher may get boldness knowing the truths God has given to him or her are more important than any nervousness. Let the desire to share God's Word with others be stronger than any nervousness or fear. If you can relate to the teaching gift, press in to some excellent teachers at your church. Watch some excellent teachers on TV or the Internet. Not only will you be getting information that will enrich your spirit and build up your faith, but you will be learning about presenting in how excellent teachers speak, lead and use the gift. Every person that has the teaching gift, is called to share those truths with others.

The teacher and those who communicate God's Word to others are held at a higher standard of accountability. This includes how we live our lives and how we use our mouths. We should be living lives of excellence and integrity. We should be speaking words that build up, encourage, edify, comfort, speaking faith and life to those around us. I am talking about accountability to God. Yes, we should have close Christian friends to speak so we can build each other up and sharpen each other (as iron sharpens iron Proverbs 27: 17) but I am saying God will hold us to a higher standard because sharing the Word of God is an awesome privilege (James 3: 1).

If you believe you have the teaching gift, press into some teachers at the church. Learn all that you can. Do some research on effective oral presentations. Do what you can to assist existing teachers that you might learn and become discipled by them. Volunteer to help with Vacation Bible School and children's Sunday school. Develop Christian friendships with those who want to talk about the things of God. Some of your best life experiences include sharing the Word of God, speaking with others of like precious faith. There is joy in Christians talking about the things of God.

Exhortation

This gift of exhortation is the desire to encourage, build up, strengthen, share words that cause others to be encouraged. This person is motivated to say kind things, special words anointed by God. The encourager is necessary in the Body of Christ. He or she will have the exact correct words to speak. Often there is a scripture or series of Scriptures. God inspires the person as he or she is talking with you. They will especially be drawn to people who are praying for an answer but have not received the answer yet. Or it could be someone who needs to hear an answer from

God because of a situation. The encourager is friendly and excellent with people. He or she gravitates towards people. Usually he or she is given words of wisdom (God giving the words that only God could know to that person) or words of knowledge (answers to situations).

A People Person

The exhorter will be well known in the church for his or her friendliness or encouraging words. Sometimes the encourager can see a solution to a situation in your life with steps or ways to get out of a tough spot. The encourager can be anointed to give wise counsel. All of this usually occurs as you serving alongside him or her at the church or during an event or outing. Exhorting others is a necessary gift. Encouragement causes hope to rise, expectation to rise and faith to be birthed. Many people in the church have this gift.

These people usually know the exact words to say to comfort, strengthen and encourage you to believing God for a promise. It can be comfort at a funeral, or kind words to someone going through a divorce or words that impart faith to someone living through a tough spot in life.

God gives the Words

God will give you words to compliment, to build up and encourage others. They are not mere words such as "Your hair looks nice" but often have to do with others spiritual gifts or callings. Usually, in Christian weddings, there is a sharing of the best qualities of the people getting married. Often there are blessings spoken over the individuals and sometimes the couple. Some of it might be prophecy, but what I am referring to here is encouraging words. They often include scriptures that you will receive as precious gems.

Should you feel a prompting to encourage someone, and you know that person needs encouragement, but you do not know what to say, pray and ask God to quicken a scripture to you. Hug the person. Express the love of God with your spirit leading. Oh yes, God can quicken words of encouragement through you that are as rays of light to someone. You may become friends with this person or it may be a time occurrence. You may develop a temporary closeness to this person as you sow continuously hope and faith and encouragement into a person's life. It might be a person you only see once and don't really know. Your sharing with that person can have eternal significance. The encourager usually gives examples of other people who have overcome similar situations. The encourager almost always shares his or her person testimony of God's faithful answer to prayer in his or her life or in others' lives. It is these personal testimonies that often touch the heart of the person needing the encouragement.

Sometimes the encourager sends cards with scriptures to shut ins or those the LORD brings to him or her. Sometimes, the encourager gives a gift with a note sharing how the person is valued.

Often you are to encourage those in your family. You are to speak to your parents or your children or your spouse. God gives us Christian families so we can build up and strengthen each other. Parents can be key figures in building up and encouraging their children. You can cheer your child into greatness. You can speak words that motivate release hope. We should also be praying to encourage our friends and associates. The gift is spiritual. It's not simply saying nice things. The impression to speak the Word comes from God and the words themselves come from God. The result is that God uses you to strengthen the deepest part of someone else – in the spirit.

The opposite of this is using your mouth to criticize and insult. In such situations, the person is speaking from the flesh words that tear down or try to insult a person. Don't even do it as a joke. Don't let negative words come out of your mouth. Foolish words or unkind words can bruise or wound a person. Remember that you will give answer for every word you speak (Matthew 12:36- 37). You can something positive instead of a joke that involves foolish words. You know the idiom, if you can't say something positive, don't speak. This should never be true of a Christian. We have hope in Christ so, we should always have an encouraging word to speak to someone.

If the friends you are with use this form of joking saying negative things to you, you need to address them and ask them not to say it anymore. If they persist in saying unkind or foolish things, you need to get with some different friends. If you don't have a friend you can pray with, you don't have a true Christian friend. Even if you are playing sports, your desire should be to be sportsmanlike – giving your best and doing your best unto God with a positive attitude.

Giving

All Christians are givers to some degree. We give our tithes and offerings to God with joy. Give generously. Give with simplicity not drawing attention to yourself. The person with the gift of giving enjoys giving financially to further the gospel. This is his or her primary passion. The giver is someone who obeys God with his or her finances. The giver gives the tithe to church but gives more. The giver is usually given special ability by God to generate funds. He or she can make money quickly.

The person is good with money. The person feels a prompting of the LORD to give and obeys. Sometimes, the person will give radically. I know of people who have given cars to people, given their house to the build the church fund etc. This is radical giving. It is in obedience to God and God always blesses that person with more.

There are also special offerings the giver may give to. If the local church needs a new roof, the giver will feel compelled to give towards this. Usually, the giver does not draw attention to himself or herself. Sometimes, the giver will want to be anonymous, so he or she will do a match funding. The giver likes to use his or her money to compel others to give. If you will give 100 dollars, the giver will match your money dollar for dollar. The person uses his or her gift to motivate others to give. Givers are motivated to give by the Holy Spirit. Sometimes God will prompt the person with a huge amount.

The giver obeys the Holy Spirit. I know of people that literally carry thousands of dollars in their pockets and give 100 dollar bills to people in the name of the LORD. I know of givers who use it as a form of evangelism. For instance, is someone is admiring a piece of jewelry but doesn't quite have the money, the giver will buy it for that person n the name of Christ.

All of us need to pray that God will bless us with more than enough finances so we can give to the gospel. I have known of people who work a second job so he or she can finance giving. We, as Christians, should make giving to the gospel a top priority because if we don't give to the gospel – no one will. Don't expect non- believers to finance the gospel. God blesses us with finances so that we can live abundantly but also that we can establish His covenant in the earth. (Deuteronomy 8: 18). We should pray that God would make us givers that are used for His glory.

We are to give to send others who will go and preach Christ throughout all the nations of the earth. Jesus promised that the gospel would be preached in all the earth before His second coming (Matthew 24: 14). It would be good if we all could go as missionaries, but some of us have jobs and situations that don't allow it. That doesn't mean we ignore the great commission. It means we give to others who do go. There are thousands of reputable missionaries and ministries that preach Christ all over the earth. Reputable ministries post on the Internet or send you where the money is spent and what is done with the money you give. They do all things keeping not only the government standard but the highest standards of accountability to God.

Becoming a Partner in Giving

You can never give to every need. Pray and let God place ministries on your heart. If there are missionaries from your church, that would be a good place to start. Should you receive inspiration from TV evangelists who are also ministries, you should give to those ministries. If we receive spiritual blessing from ministries, we should desire to help them reach more people.

God will place certain core ministries that you will want to give to. It doesn't mean you can't give special offerings elsewhere. Giving to these ministries is more than financial but it does include finances. It means you pray for them and care about them and their partners. You will care about their families. You join yourselves to them as a partner.

Please don't think becoming a partner is just giving money. It means joining your life to that ministry and caring for it as though you belong. You do belong if you believe the same that ministry believes. You do belong if they preach and teach things that encourage you spiritually. I could tell you to give to all the ministries that I feel to give to but that wouldn't be right. God Himself will impress upon your spirit ministries that I might have never have even heard of.

There are Christian motorcycle evangelists; there are Christian clown evangelists; there are Christian artists and athletes. As diverse as the population and leisure activities and ethnicities and talents, so different ministries evangelize all different types of people. Some are called to support huge ministries; others will feel to support one ministry. The director of the giving is the Holy Spirit. Your obedience is your choice. Your faithfulness is what is important. A giver will not be trying to avoid giving. A giver will feel so strongly about the work of God, he or she will be searching for ministries and people to give to. He or she will be praying for more finances so that more can be given.

1 Corinthians 9: 11 If we have sown for you spiritual things, is it a great thing if we shall reap your material things?

Be Generous

Even if you didn't score high in the gift of giving, you should be kind, generous, hospitable, caring towards those in your life. First, you should do it because that is exactly how God treats us. God always supplies more than enough. It gives God pleasure to give us the desires of our hearts. You represent Christ to people in your life – those who know you are a Christian and those who don't. Giving to others, releases thanksgiving. In those people towards God (2 Corinthians 9: 11-12).

Leadership

The ability to bring order in a group of people is a characteristic of a leader. If you are in a room with several people and something occurs that requires action, do you act and take the lead? For example, if there are people waiting in a room and there is a delivery made – but the secretary doesn't come, do you do something because someone must do something. Usually the best leaders are people who don't say ``Why me? But, ``Why not me? `` If you can do something to organize people for projects and events and you enjoy doing it and you are successful at it, you are a leader.

As with all the gifts, the proof is in the fruit. Do people follow you? If you are a leader, there will be people who want to support you and encourage you to do it because it is for their benefit. Pastors who are leaders have sheep that are happy. The church is organized in projects and successful for events. I am talking about leading not only in church though, also you could be captain of your football team or most valuable player. You could be a manager at work or the president of a company. Leaders at best are faithful and diligent. If they are not, it shames all the community. A true leader sets an example for others.

The ideas you suggest as solutions, are considered and effective. You know the gifts in the people you choose. You want what is best for everyone. These are characteristics of a leader. The spiritual leader is really a servant of God who does what is best for everybody. A secular leader in our society is appointed by people – usually by vote. You can impact not only your generation but those who are youth or children. You can influence those who witness your actions and although you don't know them personally, they know God is using you. I am saying your circles of influence can be larger than you personally know. A good leader is most valuable. You can affect the people spiritually by your participation; you can cause them to want to know Christ. Examples of these are entertainers, singers, actors, sports heroes. People don`t have to learn from mistakes if they have a strong leader. The leader chooses a wise way, the best way. You can teach by leading. The choices you make cause others to make choices.

Leaders Can Affect Nations

Leaders can speak and turn the tide of a nation with their words. Martin Luther King impacted not only the generation of the 1960`s in the USA but all of North American history from the 1960`s on. Jesus is the greatest leader, while he was on earth thousands of people followed Him to hear Him talk about God. Please take note, thousands of people followed Him even though there were no microphones, or cushy sanctuary seats. People would go into the desert or by the sea shore to hear Him speak. In His three years of public ministry, He did more miracles, touched more life and made life transforming history that continues to impact lives today.

Pastors usually stay with a congregation for all their lives. Some leaders are voted in and are there temporarily leading a nation or an organization. Certain leaders stand out in history because of how they kept their calm and brought peace and hope to their nation in the midst of a tough season. I am not political but I can still see the face of George Bush President of the USA on September 11, 2001. He had words of comfort and hope and the assurance that they as a nation would recover. His voice brought comfort beyond all party politics. There were no critics of the president that day. It was as though everyone realized the threat against the USA that day was against all of our core beliefs and freedoms (Democracy).

True leaders care about what is best for all the people – not only the people who agree with him or her. For instance, at a certain period in my life I was evangelizing almost every person I met and many of these people were either getting saved or saying they wanted to go to a church that wasn`t boring. I knew they couldn`t all come to my church. I surveyed the choices and recommended churches for them to go to and ministries for them to watch or listen to. I wanted what was best for them caring about convenience as well as their spiritual needs.

Mercy

Mercy is like empathy. It is literally feeling what the other person feels. If someone is rejoiceful and happy, the mercy will rejoice with that person. It is beyond compassion – it knits your heart to those people concerning that thing. Mercies often have strong testimonies of what God has done for them. They use these testimonies to encourage and strengthen people who are in some way needing of comfort. This can include those who are divorced, those who have lost loved ones, those who are in poverty or loss. The mercy is someone who gravitates directly to those people. They will want to speak words of comfort, impart a scripture, pray with them or give to in some way relieve suffering.

True mercies intercede for these people also knowing only God can bring true healing. The mercy should do it with cheerfulness. That is although the mercy will cry with those who are weeping, he or she shouldn't stop there. A person with a developed gift of mercy will also pray with the bereaved or speak words of encouragement. The person will most often be praying (on the inside – God give me something to say to that person). The gift of mercy is to comfort, support, build up strengthen and show compassion towards those suffering. The mercy will sometimes have assignments with people. That is while a person is recovering from a divorce, the mercy may become close friends with that person. It may be temporary or it may be permanent. The mercy must avoid living in the flesh believing that he or she is what is needed. The person must realize that Christ alone is the true hope of that person.

I would describe the motivation of mercy as an iceberg ministry. That is 1/3 of the compassion, kinds words and actions are shown to the other person, and 2/3 of the action is the prayer and prayer support of that person done privately. The purpose for the relationship is so that the mercy can speak hope and faith to the person causing his or her spirit to believe God for healing or a miracle. If you don't know what to say but you know God wants you to show mercy, start praying in tongues. God will quicken scriptures to you. If God lets you feel what another person is feeling, it's not for no reason. It is so you can make a difference. Do it with cheerfulness. Do it for the glory of God.

So What?

Which of these areas do you relate to or feel strongly that is how God is using you already or how God wants to use you? I am attaching the Spiritual Gifts Inventory. Please do it and consider getting a more in depth teaching of Spiritual Gifts. Pray for God to lead you and use you. Just as your talents and education make a career path for you, so do your spiritual gifts and developing the, shape your life. It is so important that you obey the LORD and use your spiritual gifts and your talents in all areas of your life. God wants to reach people through you. You must know your gifts and talents and you have got to grow in them to effectively reach the people God wants you to reach. You have spheres of influence no one else has.

Press into people that are mature and learn all you can. Pray over yourself. Stir up the gifts of the Spirit and expect God to use you.

MOTIVATIONAL GIFTS INVENTORY

On a Scale of 1 – 5 with 1 being low and 5 being high record your totals of the truth of these statements:

1. __Hypocrisy in yourself or others really bothers you.
2. __You help complete other people's projects before finishing your own.
3. __You speak all you know about a topic while having a conversation with someone.
4. __You have examples of people that God is growing? You use these personal examples while preaching or teaching or sharing with others.
5. __You are a good money manager and wise with money.
6. __If You are receiving or giving instructions, you want them very specific.
7. __You like to stay at home rather than be with large groups of people.
8. __You often make judgements quickly.
9. __You emphasize practical needs.
10. __You believe scriptural truth comes first, and that human experience is applied to that truth.
11. __You become impatient with a lack of progress in those you are helping.
12. __You give by logical need rather than emotional appeal.
13. __You like to organize people or groups.
14. __People who are not sensitive to others bother you.
15. __You speak sharp words.
16. __You are persistent – even pushy- if you know you are right.
17. __You focus on details so much you may lose sight of the bigger picture.
18. __You have to be careful about motivating others for personal gain.
19. __You always give to God's work no matter how many bills you have to pay.
20. __Once you have established a goal you are persistent to achieve it.
21. __It is easy for you to get close to other people.
22. __You a confident speaker in front of groups.
23. __You genuinely, deeply care for others.
24. __ You enjoy learning, doing research and organizing facts
25. __You waste time with people who are not interested in growing

spiritually.
26. __You focus on meeting immediate material needs.
27. __You can choose clear objectives and not get stuck on the details.
28. __You are someone who can easily empathize with others.
29. __You are motivated to reveal unrighteous motives by presenting God's truth.
30. __You make personal sacrifices to meet the need of others.
31. __You would like to learn Hebrew or Greek so you could understand the Bible more.
32. __You enjoy setting courses of action to help others grow in their faith.
33. __You believe that God will prosper you so that you can give to others.
34. __You use people with gifts and talents to establish common goals.
35. __It is hard for you to be firm with others.
36. __You make quick judgements about people when you first meet them.
37. __You enjoy meeting needs that will free someone to do something else.
38. __You take notes in the services and read them afterwards.
39. __You enjoy encouraging others in their spiritual growth.
40. __You entrust finances and resources to others to further their ministry.
41. __People choose you to lead them in activities or situations.
42. __You can literally relate to a person so much you care to help him/her as much as possible?
43. __You categorize people into different kinds of groups.
44. __You like to help others whether or not you receive the credit for it.
45. __You are concerned about obtaining truth?
46. __You enjoy giving others advice.
47. __You genuinely care for needs of strangers.
48. __You focus on reaching the goal: goal oriented
49. __You rejoice when others rejoice, and weep with them who weep.
50. __You despise that which is evil.
51. __You are usually helping others.
52. __You enjoy research and in depth study.
53. __You are patient with those who are not quick to progress.
54. __If someone tells you of a physical need, you are able to make a quick decision of whether it is genuine.
55. __You like to lead or manage.
56. __You enjoy comforting those who are hurting.
57. __If you knew there were a particular sin in a congregation, you would feel you should confront them as a church?

58. __You have the ability to detect personal needs in others
59. __You enjoy researching and proving truth
60. __You prefer a one on one ministry approach.
61. __God has blessed you and prospered you so you can give to others.
62. __You like to organize and plan the activities of others to reach common goals.
63. __It easy for you to empathize with others. (feel what they feel?)
64. __You would enjoy speaking to groups.
65. __You enjoy meeting practical needs of others.
66. __You prefer a study Bible more than other translations.
67. __You want to stimulate the faith of others.
68. __You have good business sense.
69. __It is easy to establish major objectives and help those around you to understand them.
70. __If a person is hurting, it is easy for you to relate to that person.

How to score the Motivational Gifts Inventory?

Place your number score next to each of the questions; add the totals:

Totals

Prophet=   1,__ 8,__ 15__, 22,__ 29,__ 36,__ 43,__ 50__, 57,__ 64__

Server =   2,__ 9,__ 16__, 23__, 30__, 37__, 44__, 51,__ 58__, 65__

Teacher =   3,__ 10,__ 17__, 24, __31,__ 38__, 45,__ 52,__ 59,__66__

Exhorter –   4,__ 11, __18,__ 25,__ 32,__ 39,__ 46,__ 53,__ 60,__ 67__

Giver -   5,__ 12,__ 19,__ 26,__ 33,__ 40,__ 47,__ 54,__ 61,__ 68__

Ruler -   6,__ 13,__ 20,__ 27,__ 34,__ 41,__ 48,__ 55, __62,__ 69__

Mercy –   7, __14, __21, __28, __35, __42, __49,__ 56,__ 63,__ 70__

Add up your totals for your gifts. Give your totals.

1. What are your predominant 3 or 4 gifts?

2. What are some characteristics about you that are a complete direct match with those gifts?

3. What Biblical characters you most identify with ? Why?

- With Reference to the Spiritual gifts Inventory from Bethesda Missionary Temple, Detroit, MI (Ann Beall 1981)

After you have completed the Inventory and have your top 3 or 4 motivational gifts, you may directly read about those gifts in the chapters that follow. They will give you traits, information on using them, Biblical examples, and hopefully encourage you to develop and use your spiritual gifts

I also highly recommend that you read the other motivational gifts to help you understand others in the body of Christ and why they do what they do. It will hopefully help us to help each other and strengthen each other as members of the Body of Christ.

3 PART THREE

Discovering More About Yourself: Manifestational Gifts of the Holy Spirit

This chapter is about recognizing God's desire to use you in the manifestational gifts. Although there are diverse expressions that God uses us in, they are all of the Holy Spirit. They are given to us as gifts; they are to be used to minister within the Body of Christ and in other parts of our lives; they are effective in quickening us to do the will of God in special situations. These special situations I term Divine Connections – moments of destiny. We can obey the prompting of the Holy Spirit at such moments and our obedience has eternal reverberations.

1 Corinthians 12: 7 But the manifestation of the Spirit is given to everyone for the common good. 8 To one is given by the Spirit the word of wisdom, to another the word of knowledge by the same Spirit, 9 to another faith by the same Spirit, to another gifts of healings by the same Spirit, 10 to another the working of miracles, to another prophecy, to another discerning of spirits, to another various kinds of tongues, and to another the interpretation of tongues. 11 But that one and very same Spirit works all these, dividing to each one individually as He will.

A manifestation is an expression of a gift or an occurrence that is evidence of something. Someone who was present could certainly say "Something has happened." No one who was there could deny something occurred because there was spiritual and physical demonstration of it. For example, in the Church service that I am familiar with, we worship God with all of our being: spirit, soul and body. Some people dance; some people kneel in praise/prayer; some people clap their hands. Some people bring instruments from home and play in the congregation, joining with the choir and worship leaders and musicians and orchestra.

Often there is such a tremendous moving of the Holy Spirit, during the praise and worship, that some people lie face down prostrate on the ground, trembling in the presence of God. Other people might be weeping. The children felt such a tug at their hearts that they would go to the front of the church and dance and wave their hands singing and dancing in worship. During the praise and worship and soaking in of the Spirit of God, no one cut it off. I mean the prime purpose we gathered was to worship and praise. No one leading was checking his or her watch. The priority was total abandonment to God that He might be glorified in our midst. He is the reason we gathered together.

The worship leaders followed the leading of the Holy Spirit and sometimes would lead with repentance; always with reverence and awe; sometimes with shouting and dancing triumphantly etc. All of these are expressions of the Holy Spirit moving in God's people. The pastors were worshipping God; the parents, the children – all the congregation was worshipping God. The presence of God was so strong there that people could receive healings, answers to prayer. Almost always there was prophecy and tongues and interpretation of tongues present. The Holy Spirit was leading the service by prompting the Body of Christ.

1 Corinthians 14: 26 How is it then, brothers? When you come together, every one of you has a psalm, a teaching, a tongue, a revelation, and an interpretation. Let all things be done for edification.

The New Song

The Holy Spirit would move on people and people would go to the altar praying and praising and worshipping. Others would make an altar there at their seat and be completely immersed in worship. Often, we would be singing the new song of the LORD (Revelation 5: 9; 14: 3). That is the Holy Spirit would move in such a way that everyone was worshipping God in freedom with a personal expression of love to God. Often, we would be singing in tongues. God would move, usually on the worship leader, and a melody would come that no one had known before – all the church worshiping with this new song. I've been a part of some churches where God would also give words in English to the song that had never been sung before.

This is different from the gift of tongues where an interpretation is required. This singing in tongues was a personal expression of love and devotion to God – simultaneously throughout the congregation. Not only as individuals but as a corporate expression of the Church we were uniquely praising and worshipping, offering our all to God. There was complete unity. This type of atmosphere that I am explaining of reverence and honour to God is an atmosphere where the Holy Spirit will use people in the manifestational gifts of the Spirit to build up and encourage the Body of Christ.

The Gift of Tongues

If you have not yet been baptized in the Holy Spirit speaking in other tongues, the good news is you can be. It is for all Christians.

Acts 2: 38 Peter said to them, "Repent and be baptized, every one of you, in the name of Jesus Christ for the forgiveness of sins, and you shall receive the gift of the Holy Spirit. 39 For the promise is to you, and to your children, and to all who are far away, as many as the Lord our God will call."

The Baptism of the Holy Spirit is Part of the Blessing of the New Covenant

God promises to give us this gift as part of the blessings of the New Covenant. Before Jesus came, in the Old Covenant with Moses and the commandments of God, there had to be an animal slain for a person's sins. It didn't erase the sins but is was an act of contrition or repentance that was with the cost of an animal's life. In the New Testament, with Jesus dying on the cross for our sins, we who believe can have our sins completely blotted out as though they never existed. It can only happen by faith in the death, burial and resurrection of Jesus Christ. We don't ever have to sacrifice animals. Instead we give offerings of praise and worship, thanking Him that we are His people.

The Gift of Tongues

If you do not have the gift of tongues, you can! Ask God for the gift. The Baptism of the Holy Spirit with the evidence of speaking in other tongues comes as we worship God; words that are not your natural language will come to; you must speak them out. As you speak them, they will flow. It is like turning on a tap. Once you first turn it on, there is a trickle, a flow and if you turn it on all the way – the water gushes out. The more you pray and praise in tongues, the more you will have a strong flow of tongues.

1 Corinthians 14: 2 For he who speaks in an unknown tongue does not speak to men, but to God. For no one understands him, although in the spirit, he speaks mysteries

As you are praying and praising in tongues, you are worshipping God. Also you are building up your spirit man. You are a spirit; you have a soul and you live in the body God gave to you. Your spirit man is the person God speaks to. As you pray in the spirit and praise in the Spirit, you build up, strengthen and quicken your spirit man. This spiritual manifestation has results as your gifts are often released.

1 Corinthians 14: 27 If anyone speaks in an unknown tongue, let it be by two, or at the most by three, and each in turn, and let one interpret. 28 But if there is no interpreter, let him remain silent in the church, and let him speak to himself and to God.

The Gift of Tongues in a Language Never Learned

Sometimes the gift of tongues will come special in a way that you will be speaking an earthly language you have never learned. My former pastor had a special gifting that as He was praising and speaking in tongues, he would sometimes be prophesying in Spanish even though he had never studied it at that point in his life. The Spanish congregation members would speak to him interpreting what he had said. He did not know until them revealed it to him.

There was a missionary about 100 years ago who ministered in China. She was born in North America but she believed she was to go to China. She had no idea how she would communicate with the people, but she obeyed the promptings of the Holy Spirit and travelled to China. As she stood on the ground in China, she began speaking in tongues. People gathered around her and were compelled to listen. She was speaking in tongues in perfect Mandarin. She had a miraculous ministry in China.

At one of my former churches, a well-respected woman minister began to speak in tongues during the praise and worship. She was to preach that day. Someone in the congregation yelled out : "She's telling. She is telling" and got up and ran out of the church. Later, it was explained to the woman who spoke in tongues that she was speaking Italian (she had never studied Italian) and she was revealing a secret to give the person a chance to repent.

The gift of tongues in the church is evidence the church is a living organism. The gifts of the Spirit in the Church are evidence to those who come in our midst that God lives in us and uses us. Also, of course it encourages the whole church body as one member obeys and speaks in tongues or interprets.

As a child, I would see my mum lying on the couch and not moving. It scared me. I had learned about death because of animals. I hated it. I would go up to my mum and hug her and sometimes cry out. She was sleeping. She explained to me that as long as I could see her breathing, I could see her chest rising, her body going up and down slightly, I should always know she was alive. It comforted me so much.

As sure as breath in a person is evidence of life, tongues and interpretation of tongues is an indicator of life in the church.

The Way of Spirit

If you are not baptized in the Holy Spirit but want to flow in the other gifts, you should first pray for the baptism of the Holy Spirit. God baptized the disciples in the Holy Spirit so that they might preach the gospel throughout the world. Think of it this way – 120 people who gathered on the day of Pentecost were baptized with the Holy Spirit and they reached people. They had no media ministry. They wrote letters by hand; they had no printing presses; they had no TV or Internet. The way to reach the whole earth is by being filled with the Holy Spirit to overflowing.

There is a way of Spirit. It is contrary to the way of sin and hell and death. The way of the Spirit is the high calling of God on your life. It is what God wants for you. Do you want to go the way of Spirit? Should you choose it, your life will never be boring. You will know the presence of God and God will use you to reach people for His glory. Use the gift of tongues to pray for yourself each day. As you pray in the Spirit, you strengthen your inner man – the spirit man.

The Gift of Interpretation of Tongues

Should you speak in tongues by the prompting of the Holy Spirit in a church service or gathering, someone must interpret it. It might be you or it could be someone else. By the moving of the Holy Spirit, the person will receive a revelation of what God wants to communicate to the people in the language of the people. If you have given a public word in tongues in the church, start praying for God to give an interpretation to you or to someone else. You will know that God wants to use you and you will speak words that are the interpretation of the tongues spoken

The Gift of Prophecy

You may get a scripture to read to the congregation. You may quote a Scripture; you may have a word of encouragement to give the people. You might edify or release joy in the people by your words. You may release a word of comfort. You will feel a prompting of the Holy Spirit to speak a word to the people.

1 Corinthians 14: 3 But he who prophesies speaks to men for their

edification and exhortation and comfort.

If you are not sure if you should speak, don't. Write it on a piece of paper and give it to the Pastor at the end of the service. If it is a word from God, the pastor will speak it to the people and will encourage you in your faith which will give you more boldness.

Different than the Motivation of Prophesy

This is different than the motivation of prophesy. The motivation of prophesy is someone's primary reason for functioning – a strong drive and it is rarer. The gift of tongues could come upon any Christian. God can use any Christian in the gift of prophesy and the person may be a teacher or a server or some other motivational gift as their prime driving desire to serve God. Sometimes there are 2 or 3 prophecies in a service by different people. You will recognize God's anointing on it because no one will interrupt anyone. It will flow supernaturally but in order. Usually all the church responds to a prophetic word by rejoicing or saying "Amen" or praising God. The people receive the gift from God. By their words, they receive the blessing of that word of prophecy so that it can produce fruit in their lives. It could be an encouragement that the person remembers throughout the week or during the season of life.

I have been in church where the word of prophesy is so strong that it compelled me to make an altar at my seat and start praying or praising. It wasn't only me – all the congregation did it.

Don't ever be ashamed of the gift of tongues or interpretation or prophecy. People who may be visiting us that do not know God or are not familiar with the gifts of the Holy Spirit, will observe and know something happened. The pastor should later explain what occurred so that all people would have understanding that God was manifesting His presence through the people.

The Gift of Faith

The gift of faith is different than faith for salvation or what you believe about God. The gift of faith is a supernatural empowering presence of God to believe God for a specific matter. Example, you may have a scripture quickened to you and you know God is speaking to you directly. You receive the word and believe it will come to pass. The gift of faith is necessary for us to receive miracles or healings. The gift of faith applied to scripture always produces spiritual fruit.

Often in church services, the prophetic word that comes ignites the gift of faith in you. This is especially true if the words are exactly what you needed to hear. You will have a sense of it. You will know God is using that person to speak hope and faith to you.

God's word is the way to release faith in your home or your private life. Read the promises of God out loud. Say them; pray them; receive them as yours and confess them. Thank God for manifesting the answer to you even before you see the results. It is an energizing supernatural force within in you that is stronger than anything on earth – the gift of faith.

Some people have specific faith for healings or for answers to prayer or for buildings (for the church). It is God quickening the person in the inner man to believe stronger than any natural force.

If you are in the congregation and you feel the gift of faith rise up, respond. An example could be a preacher giving a message on healing and you feel a strong belief that the word of God is for you personally, do what God is prompting you to do. It might mean going forward and praying at the altar. It might means raising your hands in worship. You will know the gift of faith is quickened to you because you will believe for the miraculous knowing that God can do it. Any doubt or fear will be totally gone. You will believe and it is this type of faith that the woman who touched the hem of Jesus garment had.

Luke 8: 46 But Jesus said, "Someone touched Me, for I perceive that power has gone out from Me." 47 When the woman saw that she was not hidden, she came trembling. And falling down before Him, she declared to Him before all the people why she had touched Him and how she was healed immediately. 48 Then He said to her, "Daughter, be of good cheer. Your faith has made you well. Go in peace."

The faith that she had that day was not natural faith in God or even in Jesus. She knew that she knew if she could just touch the hem of Jesus robe, she would be healed.

It Could be You

As with any of these gifts – it may be personal for you or it may be prophetic where you believe it is for the whole church. You might get the gift of faith for yourself (most usual) or you may get a prophetic sense that God wants to heal people that day. What you should do is either speak to the pastor but if he or she is preaching, speak to an usher and get him or her to get a message to the pastor. It is awesome when the Pastor gets a gift of faith for healing but please know, it could come from you. God may prompt you will a strong knowing that God wants to heal people that day. Do not interrupt the service. If you cannot get the message to the pastor during the service, approach him or her afterwards.

Often the gift of faith is present for the gifts of healing or working of miracles to be manifest.

Gifts of Healing

There are people who have been given the gifts of healing. They will speak words that promote faith and they will announce that God wants to heal. Mostly it is the pastor, but it could from an elder or a member of the congregation who is used by God that day. The person will have a strong sense that God wants to heal people. Age is not the determiner of the gift. Your spiritual gifts grow by you using them and learning to obey the promptings of the Holy Spirit.

Usually, the person will announce things such as God wants to heal people with Diabetes or pain in the back etc. As the person calls out (using the gift of words of knowledge) the areas pf healing, your symptom may be mentioned. You will get a strong sense God wants to heal you and you will go forward for healing prayer. Sometimes no one lays hands on you at all. Sometimes, healing comes as soon as you step towards the front of the church.

Sometimes, you can be healed by prayer and the laying on of hands of the pastor or altar workers. As they are praying, you are completely healed. It may be immediate. Sometimes it is gradual. You may feel the presence of God, but later you realize there is no pain at all and you are healed. It could be physical healing. It could be inward healing. You may be able to forgive someone and release any negative feeling you had about someone who abused you or said things about you. God can bring healing to your spirit, soul, body.

Sometimes, people kind of manifest a special area in the gifts. It isn't as though they planned it but is was the truth. I knew one pastor who would pray for barren women and they would have children. It occurred more than once. If God is using you to pray and healings occur, get on the prayer team. You should be using that gift regularly. It was almost as if God were directing the women to him for healing. It was God using that pastor through the gift of healing.

There is nothing that people can't be healed of because Jesus Christ paid the price for our healing. Just like he died for our sins, he took upon him all sickness and disease so that by faith we could receive healing. There is no sickness Jesus cannot heal.

My Testimony of Healing

I myself received a miraculous instantaneous healing in my foot. I had twisted my ankle and it was swollen and purple. It was hard to walk, but I went to church anyway. I stood (it was faith that let me stand because I could feel the pain). As the worship service began, praise and worship, was triumphant and it released worship within me. I heard a voice within me that said would you believe? I was leaning on the chair in front of me. My heart responded with joy. I was worshipping God and I chose to worship over the pain. Faith was ignited in my spirit and I began to dance for God. I was dancing on that foot and I didn't feel any pain. I danced and rejoiced throughout the service. No one gave an altar call for healing. Only God ignited the faith in me. I was healed completely – because of the atmosphere of praise and worship and my decision to worship.

Working of Miracles

I have only witnessed this gift on TV or on the Internet or Christian DVDS. It includes things such as a lame person being about to walk; a blind person being about to see; a deaf person being able to heal, a hand that was withered that grows miraculously to be normal. These types of miracles are predominant in ministries in Africa, Asia, India etc. Most Missionary Evangelists have the gift of faith for this gift to be manifest. After someone is miraculously healed, thousands who came to the event but perhaps were not saved are saved, and some of them also healed or made whole.

The working of miracles is a gift that has two parts to it. The gift of faith comes very strong and a preacher or person who demonstrates this gift will often say "Do what you couldn't do". What you will do is respond in faith. It is like the first faith that was quickened in your heart to accept Jesus as your Saviour. You knew that you should. It is that same type of strong faith that will be quickened in your heart to believe for a miracle. It could be a physical miracle. I have known of people who were healed and were blind but could see. I have heard of people who were lame but could walk. Such miracles occur because of faith and obedience. They took a step of faith. They acted on their faith. They obeyed the prompt to do what they couldn't do and waved their hands or got up.

The working of miracles has an element where you do something to show your faith and in it you are healed. My own mother who could barely walk because of arthritis obeyed an altar call at church and I went with her to pray for her. As the pastor prayed for her, she was slain in the spirit. I kneeled and covered her with a blanket and also prayed for her. She got up and began running. She gave her testimony from the platform. She obeyed the prompting of faith and received healing.

Some examples of people who have flowed in this gift strongly are T. L. Osborn, Smith Wigglesworth, Charles and Francis Hunter and others.

Word of Wisdom

Sometimes God will give you wisdom about a situation or a person you know nothing about naturally. You will feel that you should say it. There will be a prompting of the Holy Spirit for you to say it. If you do not feel the prompting to say it – don't. Sometimes God may give you information or allow you to see things about people, but it is not for you to speak it to those people.

I have been in meetings where the preacher or teacher gets a word of wisdom for someone and the person runs to the front and makes an altar to God acknowledging the Word was from God. The wisdom is something you couldn't possibly know with your human intellect and can guide the person into making a choice or solving a problem. God can use others in the gift – especially with your family and friends but also in your youth group or small group at Church. It could occur during a church altar call where people are praying for each other. As you are praying, you say something you hadn't planned to say and what occurs is the person knows it is a word of wisdom from God – the answer to a situation he or she has been praying about.

The word of wisdom may often come to someone with the gift of encouragement. As that person is speaking with you, he or she speaks words that not only strengthen you but often the person gets a solution – in the form of steps or points to follow to get out of the situation. As the encourager gives you the word, your inner man or heart will agree – saying yes – yes. I believe this. If you do not have that inner witness, do not proceed or let the person pray for you. God will never speak to you through someone without your inner most being agreeing. You will recognize it is God speaking through that person; you will accept it.

Word of Knowledge

The Word of knowledge can come to people ministering to you. Usually, it is given by someone praying for them. What it is that God reveals some private fact about you that no one else knows. The person ministering you gets a glimpse of it (it can be visual) or gets an impression in his or her spirit about you and knows something intimate and private about you. A sure sign this is from God is the person never accuses you or condemns you or says anything that would affect you negatively. How you know it is from God is this way. The person will say it. You will immediately know without a doubt there is no way that person could know it. You will understand God is speaking through that individual. Usually, the word of knowledge quickens faith in you so strongly that you believe for whatever it is you are praying about.

It can occur at the altar with someone praying with you. I once had a pastor who was a prophet of God and often he would get words of wisdom and words of knowledge for people in the congregation as he was preaching. He would often call them to come forward and he would speak the word. Usually he or she or they would either be slain in the spirit (fall down worshipping God) or kneel in prayer. Sometimes, they would shout and thank God for the word. There was an outward sign that they received the word. Usually, the pastor would pray for them and prophesy over them afterwards. People who flow in the prophetic usually flow in the gift of word of wisdom or word of knowledge.

I have had words of wisdom, words of knowledge spoken over me as people were praying over me. What it does is build your faith and cause you to press into God more because you realize God is speaking through the person to you. The key is that you know without a doubt only God and you knew that information and the person praying over you is hearing from God.

You will know you are speaking a word of wisdom or knowledge over someone because the person will say "yes, it is true" and accept the word.

If you do not Feel Inward Peace or an Inner Witness

Please realize just are there are false diamonds, diamonds that are really just glass, there are false people who may even be in the church and at the altar. The person may something to you – if you do not feel a strong inner witness – don't accept it. Some people are trying to use their gifts and they might make a mistake as they are learning how to obey the Holy Spirit. Unfortunately, also there are false gifts. I have not encountered it very much but I have. I would back away from the person and pray and confess – I do not accept that word. Even if it seems rude, back away. I would rather appear rude than come into agreement with something I don't agree with that can affect my life.

Discerning of Spirits

Once someone becomes a Christian, one of the things I highly recommend he or she ides is start praying for discernment. All Christians have some level of discerning of spirits. It is the ability to discern if it is God's Holy Spirit or discern some evil spirit. People that have the gift of discerning of spirits can often recognize the demon and cast it out. People who have this gift often sense the presence of God and revere God so much that they will stay in God's presence for hours worshipping and honouring Him.

After I was saved, (I was not raised in a Christian home) I kept doing most of what I had been doing but the second day of my salvation a profound thing occurred. I realized that the books and teachings I had on the occult had to be burned. I knew by the Spirit of God I had to throw them out but that wasn't enough. I burned them. I had invested hundreds of dollars into those materials. It had to be the Spirit of God moving on me to get rid of those things. I knew clearly they had to be burned. I was choosing Christ. I would have no other gods. Afterwards, I told the people who had led me to the LORD what happened, and they showed me in the scripture where in the book of Acts the exact thing occurred (Acts 19: 15). I began to know the prompting of the Holy Spirit letting me know what was good for me and what would only harm me.

Obey or Learn to Obey

I was watching the movies our family had always watched – scary vampire movies that are still quite popular today. I felt the prompting of the Holy Spirit on me to turn it off that it wasn't good for me. I wish I could tell you I obeyed. I did not. I said within myself 'I have always watched these types of shows. I can do whatever I want." Afterwards, I was in bed and it was as though evil spirits kept attacking me. The movie was more than scary. It was of the kingdom of darkness. Before I had known Christ, I was living in that darkness, but once I became a child of the light, I could no longer tolerate the darkness. I repented and begged God to forgive me and I obeyed the Holy Spirit concerning these things: movies: media etc.

What we take into our eyes, our ears, our hearts – goes into our life. Choose wisely what you place into your being. You are a vessel of God – the most Holy – the most awesome. If you want God to use you, you cannot live in the world's darkness and be a child of the light. You cannot do the same things as those who are sinning and expect to see God use you in the gifts of the spirit.

Romans 12: 1-2 I urge you therefore, brothers, by the mercies of God, that you present your bodies as a living sacrifice, holy, and acceptable to God, which is your reasonable service of worship. 2 Do not be conformed to this world, but be transformed by the renewing of your mind, that you may prove what is the good and acceptable and perfect will of God.

Don't just give your life to Christ once and do whatever you want. You can and I'm not doubting that God is merciful and if you believe in Jesus blood shed for you would be saved. True Christians are not trying to find ways to live fleshly lives and live as close to hell on earth as they can. True Christians will seek Christ despising their own sin and pray "God teach me to love the things you love and hate the things you hate." Even if you are not from a Christian home, God can radically transform you by His Word, His Spirit and His blood. It is called sanctification. God helps you to be transformed so you love what is good for you and hate what is evil.

How to Grow Your Gifts

You use the gifts, you exercise the gifts, you develop them by obeying the promptings of the Holy Spirit. If you make a mistake, the Holy Spirit will correct you or a pastor or an elder in the church will correct you. Don't let it stop you. After the service, go speak with the pastor or elder and find out how you missed it. Ask what part wasn't correct. Get instruction. We learn best from those who are mature and who will speak honestly. In most services where I have heard correction given, it is given with love and caring and the reason it is not appropriate is mentioned. It isn't focused on more than that. The pastor or elders can sense if you are earnestly trying to use your gifts or if you are falsely trying to harm the people.

The more you use the gifts, the more proficiently you use them. It is awesome should there be a leader man or woman in your life who you can learn from. That person will share with you what to avoid and what to do. A person such as this is a treasure. You can receive so much from him or her because the person has similar giftings. Press into that person.

Sometimes the person is there in your life all your life long but it has not been the case for me. I thank God for those teachers and preachers who invested in my life.

Gifts Manifest in the Church

First you must know the motivational and manifestation gifts. Understanding the functioning of the gifts helps you to know your own. As you obey the Holy Spirit's prompting, you will use your gifts and develop them. All of this usually occurs in the local church. God will put you with people who can help you to develop your gifts. The more people who know their gifts and that are living in the Spirit with God's leading, the more there will be salvation, healing, deliverance, the manifestations of God in the Church. It is not only for the pastors but it is for all of the church members to know their giftings.

Each part of the Body of Christ has something to contribute by participation in the worship service. The total presence of God in the church during a church service is more than the sum of all the parts. A spiritual dynamic happens as we Christians share using our gifts and talents that builds up, edifies, encourages and strengthens the body. It could be prophecy or tongues or interpretation of tongues, reading a scripture or any of the gifts discussed in this chapter. The key is obedience to the Holy Spirit's promptings.

Ephesians 4: 16 from whom the whole body is joined together and connected by every joint and ligament, as every part effectively does its work and grows, building itself up in love.

Every local body of Christ is slightly different. No two churches are exactly the same. That's part of why I love to visit different churches. There are certain types of praise and worship, different predominant giftings in the lead pastors, different guest speakers, a slightly different emphasis on certain key truths and different discernable fruit in the churches. At some churches, my own gifting is different than at others. It is because the Holy Spirit joins together the parts of the body of Christ that are there in new ways as Christians visit or minister.

The minister or ministers and choir and orchestra are not the only ones who should be contributing to the service as the church gathers together. God may want to use you to pray for someone or to speak to someone. It could be in the sanctuary but you can minister any place. You can impart words of encouragement to people in the entrance way or the bathroom. You can be praying for people silently; they don't even have to know you are doing it. If you truly want to serve God, go to Church not only to get something from the pastor – but see how many people you can bless with words of encouragement. If you don't know what to say. Pray, get a scripture and speak that good word to as many people as you can.

Stir up the Gifts Within you

2 Timothy 1: 6 Therefore I remind you to stir up the gift of God, which is in you by the laying on of my hands.

If you completed the spiritual Gifts Inventory, you added your totals 3 or 4 high scores show areas that are potentially areas of your strengths in these gifts. Please don't think that any survey is totally accurate – it only gives you an idea of your giftings. They may not be fully developed yet. If you see some areas that you would say that you don't identify with, it could be because it is not a predominant gift or it could be that it hasn't been developed yet.

Although you are predominant in several motivational giftings, please know Jesus Christ lives in you. All of the gifts of the Spirit are in you to some degree because Jesus has the fullness of all the gifts. The manifestational gifts are for you to use to effectively minister for Christ. If you were the only Christian in a place where there was a demand on the gift of healing, God could and would use you should you obey the promptings of the Holy Spirit. You might never be used in it again. People who have a need for healing or for an answer to prayer or whatever, who have faith place a demand on the gifts of the Holy Spirit by their faith. Their faith towards God releases God's mercy towards them. You could be the vessel God uses if you are obedient.

I would encourage you to stir up the gifts of the Spirit that are in you by literally laying hands on yourself and saying out loud "I stir the gift of...NAME IT" You are not commanding God – you are doing what God told us to do which is to stir up the gifts of the Spirit. I heard Kenneth Copeland tell a story as he was getting ready to speak at a conference, he was thinking to himself what he would do and he said within himself " I don't really feel like..." and God checked him right there and the Holy Spirit told him to stir himself up in the gifts of God.

He started saying out loud : "I stir myself up in God. I stir the gifts of the Spirit" and immediately he felt the anointing to minister. By praying and confessing over yourself, you can stir the gifts of God so that you can minister. If you do have a deep desire for God to use you, make it a practice of stirring up all the gifts of the Spirit and ask God to use you each day. Your willingness and obedience make you a candidate for God to flow through. If you can get a hold of Roberts Liardon's teaching on stirring up the gifts of the Spirit, I highly recommend it as an encouragement to you to help you stir your giftings. If you are not taught this simple truth, you may believe you have to wait for God to move upon you. Yes, God does move upon you but there is a part of you that engages with God. You can stir up yourself to press into God and to be used of God.

We Need the Gifts of the Spirit

We have the gifts of the Spirit because we need the gifts of the Spirit to witness effectively. They are not for entertainment. They are not for trophies. They are to use in the service of Jesus Christ preaching salvation, healing and deliverance. They are used to help make us effective witnesses of Christ. They encourage us as Christians as the gifts manifest in the church but they are also given to us so the gifts could be used wherever God has us: school, home, work, business etc.

Don't be content to stay at the same faith level you are at. Set your heart on Jesus and start pressing closer to Him for the rest of your life. Pray that you will be constantly growing from faith to faith (Romans 1: 17). Stir yourself up and believe that God can use you more each day. Believe that God wants to use you. God chose you. God gave you talents and gifts. God gave you motivational gifts and manifestation gifts for a purpose – for you to use. Believe that God wants to use you. Expect God to use you. Prepare by reading the word of God and praying and stirring up your gifts.

If you do not Have a Christian family

If you are the only Christian in your home, pray for your family. Claim them in prayer. Pray that God would release labourers to witness to them who they would believe. You might be the only Christian who ever loves them enough to pray for them to be saved. If your family are not Christians get some close friends who are Christians who you can pray with and use the gifts of the Spirit with. If you don't have any close Christian friends, start praying for God to give you those types of friends. Someone at church might be the person who has a gift that will encourage you or visa versa. God wants us to use our gifts to build up and strengthen each other. The plan for a Christian family is that we would use our giftings with each other. You don't have to miss out. If you do not have Christian family, God can give you Christian friends who are closer than natural family. They will pray for you and with you.

What to do with This Teaching

Build yourself up in the most Holy Faith (Jude 1: 20). Read the word of God. Go to church. Go not just to get but to give. Prayerfully commit your life to Christ continuously and expect to see Him manifest His presence in you and through you. Get some Christian media in your life. Christian broadcasting like TBN or GOD TV or DayStar or preaching and teaching from the Internet. Never believe you are alone. There are millions of Christians all over the earth who believe in Jesus Christ. Christian media connects us, encourages us and builds us up. This is especially important if you do not have a Christian family.

People will see the light of Christ on your life. If you live radically in the Spirit, praising, praying, speaking in tongues, living Holy, people will notice you. They make consider you weird, but please know if they have a prayer request, they will come to you and ask for prayer because they know you love God. Believe that God wants to use you; get Christian friends you can pray with; press as close to you can to Jesus; pray in the Holy Spirit that God would use you – every day for the rest of your life.

CONCLUSION

Never believe that your age limits you. Don't despise your youth. If you love Christ with all your being and stir up yourself in the Holy Spirit, you can live radically for Jesus Christ at any age and impact the earth for His glory. This means that not only can you pursue your natural talents and abilities for your own pleasure, and for the pleasure of others, you can be a light for Christ in your community. Through knowing your spiritual gifts and the gifts of the Spirit that God has given to the Church, you can fully pursue the career interest you desire.

The choices you make in developing your talents and gifts helps to shape and define your life. Whether it is sports or music or dance or writing, you will meet other people who pursue the same interests. You will impact different spheres of society than any other person. Your education for your career as well as the unique gifts and callings are given to you by God to equip you for your life on earth. They are ultimately to help you be a strong witness for Jesus Christ on earth. They identify you as a special person.

Keep your heart pure. Keep your life clean. Follow after righteousness. Stir up your spiritual gifts by praying for yourself. Build up yourself in the most Holy faith. That means listen to things that encourage you and strengthen your faith. Watch things that are pure and upright. Feed yourself spiritual food – preaching, teaching, Bible study. Praise God at home and throughout your day – not just at church. Revere God's Word and place it as essential as prayer as the top priority of each day.

If you have Christian parents, seek their wise counsel in all major decisions of your life. Get them to pray for you regularly if they don't already do it. Make friends with Christians who you can pray with and talk about the things of God with. Make goals for yourself. Think of the present, the next several years and also in the future what you hope for. Whatever you can imagine, you can become. Let the Word of God be your plumb line – the line against which all things must measure correctly.

Closing Prayer

May God cause you to know your talents and motivational gifts and manifestation gifts. May God give you close Christian friends who will build you up and encourage you. May God use you to minister salvation, healing and deliverance to others. I pray encouragement, strength, favour and opportunity to come to you to serve God now and all of your life. In Jesus name. Amen.

RESOURCES

List of Jobs taken from the Ontario Employment page
https://www.app.tcu.gov.on.ca/eng/labourmarket/ojf/findoccupation.asp

Go to the website. You would choose one of the following and specific
information about that opportunity will be on the page including
description, education requirements, job demand, pay etc.

Accounting and related clerks (1431)
Administrative officers (1221)
Aerospace engineers (2146)
Aircraft assemblers and aircraft assembly inspectors (9481)
Aircraft instrument, electrical and avionics mechanics, technicians and
inspectors (2244)
Aircraft mechanics and aircraft inspectors (7315)
Air pilots, flight engineers and flying instructors (2271)
Architects (2151)
Architectural technologists and technicians (2251)
Assemblers and inspectors, electrical appliance, apparatus and equipment
manufacturing (9484)
Audio and video recording technicians (5225)
Audiologists and speech-language pathologists (3141)
Automotive service technicians, truck and bus mechanics and mechanical
repairers (7321)
Bakers (6252)
Banking, credit and other investment managers (0122)
Banking, insurance and other financial clerks (1434)
Biological technologists and technicians (2221)
Biologists and related scientists (2121)
Boilermakers (7262)
Bookkeepers (1231)
Bricklayers (7281)
Butchers and meat cutters and fishmongers - retail and wholesale (6251)
Cabinetmakers (7272)
Carpenters (7271)
Chefs (6241)
Chemical engineers (2134)
Chemical Technologists and technicians (2211)
Chemists (2112)
Chiropractors (3122)
Civil engineering technologists and technicians (2231)
Civil engineers (2131)

College and other vocational instructors (4131)
Community and social service workers (4212)
Computer and Information Systems managers (0213)
Computer engineers (except software engineers) (2147)
Computer network technicians (2281)
Computer programmers and interactive media developers (2174)
Concrete finishers (7282)
Construction estimators (2234)
Construction managers (0711)
Cooks (6242)
Crane operators (7371)
Customer service, information and related clerks (1453)
Database analysts and data administrators (2172)
Dental assistants (3411)
Dental hygienists and dental therapists (3222)
Dentists (3113)
Dietitians and nutritionists (3132)
Drafting technologists and technicians (2253)
Drillers and blasters - service mining, quarrying and construction (7372)
Early childhood educators and assistants (4214)
Economists and economic policy researchers and analysts (4162)
Editors (5122)
Electrical and electronics engineering technologists and technicians (2241)
Electrical and electronics engineers (2133)
Electrical mechanics (7333)
Electrical power line and cable workers (7244)
Electric appliance servicers and repairers (7332)
Electricians (except industrial and power system) (7241)
Electronics assemblers, fabricators, inspectors and testers (9483)
Electronic service technicians (household and business equipment) (2242)
Elementary and secondary school teacher assistants (6472)
Elevator constructors and mechanics (7318)
Executive assistants (1222)
Farmers and farm managers (8251)
Financial and investment analysts (1112)
Financial auditors and accountants (1111)
Financial managers (0111)
Fire-fighters (6262)
Floor covering installers (7295)
Food and beverage servers (6453)
Forestry technologists and technicians (2223)
Funeral directors and embalmers (6272)
Gas fitters (7253)

General practitioners and family physicians (3112)
Geological and mineral technologists and technicians (2212)
Geological engineers (2144)
Geologists, geochemists and geophysicists (2113)
Glaziers (7292)
Graphic arts technicians (5223)
Graphic designers and illustrating artists (5241)
Hairstylists and barbers (6271)
Heavy-duty equipment mechanics (7312)
Heavy equipment operators (except crane) (7421)
Human resources managers (0112)
Industrial and manufacturing engineers (2141)
Industrial designers (2252)
Industrial electricians (7242)
Industrial engineering and manufacturing technologists and technicians (2233)
Industrial instrument technicians and mechanics (2243)
Information systems analysts and consultants (2171)
Inspectors in public and environmental health and occupational health and safety (2263)
Insurance adjusters and claims examiners (1233)
Insurance agents and brokers (6231)
Insurance, real estate and financial brokerage managers (0121)
Insurance underwriters (1234)
Interior designers (5242)
Ironworkers (7264)
Journalists (5123)
Landscape and horticultural technicians and specialists (2225)
Landscape architects (2152)
Land surveyors (2154)
Lawyers and Quebec notaries (4112)
Librarians (5111)
Machine fitters (7316)
Machining tool operators (9511)
Machinists and machining and tooling inspectors (7231)
Managers in health care (0311)
Manufacturing managers (0911)
Mechanical engineering technologists and technicians (2232)
Mechanical engineers (2132)
Medical radiation technologists (3215)
Medical secretaries (1243)
Medical sonographers (3216)
Metallurgical and materials engineers (2142)

Mining engineers (2143)
Motor vehicle assemblers, inspectors and testers (9482)
Motor vehicle body repairers (7322)
Non-destructive testers and inspectors (2261)
Nursery and greenhouse operators and managers (8254)
Occupational therapists (3143)
Optometrists (3121)
Other financial officers (1114)
Other professional engineers, n.e.c. (2148)
Other professional occupations in physical sciences (2115)
Other technical occupations in motion pictures, broadcasting and the performing arts (5226)
Painters and decorators (7294)
Pharmacists (3131)
Physiotherapists (3142)
Plasterers, drywall installers and finishers, and lathers (7284)
Plastics processing machine operators (9422)
Plumbers (7251)
Police officers (except commissioned) (6261)
Power system electricians (7243)
Production clerks (1473)
Property administrators (1224)
Psychologists (4151)
Purchasing agents and officers (1225)
Purchasing and inventory clerks (1474)
Purchasing managers (0113)
Real estate agents and salespersons (6232)
Refrigeration and air conditioning mechanics (7313)
Registered nursing assistants (3233)
Residential home builders and renovators (0712)
Respiratory therapists and clinical perfusionists (3214)
Restaurant and food service managers (0631)
Retail and wholesale buyers (6233)
Roofers and shinglers (7291)
School and guidance counsellors (4143)
Securities agents, investment dealers and traders (1113)
Sewing machine operators (9451)
Sheet metal workers (7261)
Shippers and receivers (1471)
Social workers (4152)
Software engineers and designers (2173)
Specialist physicians (3111)
Specialists in human resources (1121)

Steamfitters, pipefitters and sprinkler system installers (7252)
Storekeepers and parts clerks (1472)
Structural metal and platework fabricators and fitters (7263)
Supervisors, mining and quarrying (8221)
Survey technologists and technicians (2254)
Systems testing technicians (2283)
Technical sales specialists, wholesale trade (6221)
Telecommunications installation and repair workers (7246)
Tellers, financial services (1433)
Tilesetters (7283)
Tool and die makers (7232)
Translators, terminologists and interpreters (5125)
Travel counsellors (6431)
Truck drivers (7411)
Underground mine service and support workers (8411)
Underground production and development miners (8231)
Urban and land use planners (2153)
User support technicians (2282)
Veterinarians (3114)
Waterworks and gas maintenance workers (7442)
Web designers and developers (2175)
Welders and related machine operators (7265)
Writers (5121)

Chris A. Legebow

Books By the Same Author
Available on Amazon.com or Amazon.ca or Kindle

References

Legebow, C. (2016) *Discovering and using your spiritual gifts*. Windsor: ON CANADA.: Living Word.

Legebow, C. (2016) *Kinds of prayer. Knowing them and using them effectively*. Windsor ON CANADA.: Living Word.

ABOUT THE AUTHOR

Chris Legebow is a Christian Professor of English and Communications.
She has taught at the elementary, high school and College and University
levels. She has ministered in her local churches in intercessory prayer,
teaching Sunday school and other Christian Doctrine classes to children
and youths. She has preached to congregations and given her testimony.
Although she was not raised in a Christian home, she came to know Jesus
Christ as her Saviour and LORD while she was studying in University. This
radically transformed her life in terms of priorities and commitment.

She has a strong passion for the great commission – that Jesus Christ would
be preached throughout all the earth believing that it a major sign of the
LORD's return. She has been a part of several different types of full gospel
charismatic churches but has also gained much of her insight and
enlightenment from Christian Media and broadcasting. She hopes to
continue ministering, serving, interceding and giving and teaching until the
LORD returns.

www.ingramcontent.com/pod-product-compliance
Lightning Source LLC
Chambersburg PA
CBHW021213020426
42331CB00003B/340